FROM
INFERTILITY TO
IN VITRO
FERTILIZATION

FROM INFERTILITY TO IN VITRO FERTILIZATION

A PERSONAL AND PRACTICAL GUIDE TO MAKING THE DECISION THAT COULD CHANGE YOUR LIFE

GEOFFREY SHER, M.D.,

AND

VIRGINIA A. MARRIAGE, R.N., M.N.,

WITH

JEAN STOESS, M.A.

McGraw-Hill Publishing Company

New York   St. Louis   San Francisco   Bogotá
Hamburg   Madrid   Mexico   Milan   Montreal
Paris   São Paulo   Tokyo   Toronto

1 2 3 4 5 6 7 8 9 FGR FGR 8 9 2 1 0 9 8

ISBN 0-07-056761-1

Library of Congress Cataloging-in-Publication Data

Sher, Geoffrey, 1943-
  From infertility to in vitro fertilization.

  Includes index.
  1. Fertilization in vitro, Human—Popular works.
I. Marriage, Virginia A. II. Stoess, Jean. III. Title.
RG135.S54 1989   618.1'78'059   88-23120
ISBN 0-07-056761-1

Book design by Sheree Goodman

This book is dedicated to the patients of the Pacific Fertility Center, San Francisco, and of the Northern Nevada Fertility Center, Reno, and to my associate and dear friend Victor K. Knutzen, M.D., without whom the experience necessary to write this book would never have been gained.

—Geoffrey Sher, M.D.

ACKNOWLEDGMENTS

We wish to thank William Vaught, Ph.D., and Linda Vaught, Ph.D., for providing information for the section in Chapter 6 entitled "The Laboratory's Role in IVF."

We would also like to express our appreciation to the staff of the Pacific Fertility Center, San Francisco, and of the Northern Nevada Fertility Center, Reno, for their contributions to this book.

Finally, we wish to thank Dave Thomas of General Graphics, Inc., Reno, for the artwork.

CONTENTS

FOREWORD

Over the past five years, I have seen infertility from a variety of perspectives. As victim, advocate, and consumer protector, I have learned that the most critical element in a couple's journey through infertility is information. Yet for the millions of couples experiencing infertility, accurate, digestible data is difficult to find. Primarily because of this lack of information, I founded the de Miranda Institute for Infertility and Modern Parenting (dMI). Our organization strives to offer consumers the information they need to make crucial infertility decisions. In addition, the president of dMI, Carol Peters, and I serve on a national committee for insurance advocacy that advises those who are interested in passing legislation mandating insurance coverage of in vitro fertilization and gamete intrafallopian transfer.

For two years we have been answering questions about infertility, particularly questions about new reproductive technologies and insurance coverage. We rely on information we gather ourselves from many different sources. Multitudes of books exist on infertility, but none specifically addresses IVF and GIFT. All too frequently, couples rely on information they glean from a few poor sources. Although dMI attempts to remedy this situation, what is really needed is a book—and not just any book, but one that gradually builds consumer understanding of the process. That book is here, thanks to Dr. Geoffrey Sher and his coauthors, Virginia A. Marriage and Jean Stoess. The authors have put together a definitive guide to the most intimate science: the new reproductive technologies. I am very happy to see this book published and I have complete confidence in its accuracy.

Dr. Geoffrey Sher and Dr. Victor Knutzen are co-directors of the Pacific Fertility Center in San Francisco and the Northern Nevada Fertility Center in Reno, where their IVF programs have had enviable success. Most of the couples I know who have gone through IVF at these programs have felt that it was a positive experience regardless of outcome. I would have to concur as a former patient.

Infertile consumers think well of the Pacific Fertility Center in San Francisco (where Dr. Sher is currently located) and its sister clinic in Reno, because the staff is caring and concerned. It is that feeling that motivated Dr. Sher to produce this book. Every page gives clear and concise information to infertile consumers starved for straight talk. Understanding what will, might, and could occur is sometimes frightening. But not knowing anything is worse. All too often infertile couples go into treatment uncertain and unprepared. They are bewildered and frightened...hardly the state of mind associated with the joy of conception.

In this book, the most difficult aspects of treatment are stripped of jargon and served unadorned to the consumer. The authors explain how laboratories handle embryos. They also discuss the possibility of multiple births factually and clearly. Contrary to the belief among some infertile people that large multiple pregnancies are an added bonus, they can be life-threatening. A patient's age, health, physique, and blood pressure are just some of the factors that must be considered in the event of multiple pregnancy. Decisions about multiple births must be made in advance. This consumer guide allows that kind of preplanning.

Finally, the section which I counsel every infertile couple to read is the chapter on insurance coverage. Pay attention to what the authors say and get involved. Political activism is the only way to get coverage. If you are not sure you deserve coverage, ask your insurance coordinator what happens to the maternity benefits you never use.

If you are infertile or considering GIFT or IVF, read this book. You need it. I hope that in a few years there will be no need for a consumer protection agency for the infertile. Until then, educate yourself.

—Gina de Miranda
de Miranda Institute for
Infertility and Modern Parenting
Bedford, Texas

PREFACE

In vitro fertilization (IVF) has come a long way since 1978, when Louise Brown, dubbed "the world's first test-tube baby" by the press, was born in England. The first in vitro fertilization program in the United States was introduced at the Eastern Virginia Medical School at Norfolk in the late 1970s. Now, more than 180 clinics throughout this country offer IVF, with varying degrees of reported success.

In vitro fertilization literally means "fertilization in glass." Traditionally known as in vitro fertilization and embryo transfer (IVF/ET), the procedure is more commonly referred to as *in vitro fertilization,* or IVF. (The term IVF will be used throughout this book instead of the more cumbersome IVF/ET.)

IVF comprises several basic steps. First, the woman is given fertility drugs that stimulate her ovaries to produce as many mature eggs as possible. Then, when the ovaries have been properly stimulated with fertility hormones, the eggs are retrieved by suction through a needle inserted into her ovaries. The harvested eggs are then fertilized in a glass petri dish in the laboratory with her partner's or a donor's sperm. Several days later, the fertilized egg or eggs—now known as *embryos*—are transferred by a thin catheter through the woman's vagina into her uterus, where it is hoped they will grow into one or more healthy babies. (This procedure will be described in detail in Chapters 4–7.)

Although IVF is an extremely promising procedure, it is no substitute for standard, less invasive (nonsurgical) methods for treating infertility. For this reason, it is essential that the infertile couple and their physician identify the cause of the infertility in order to determine the most appropriate form of treatment. This does not mean that IVF should be regarded as a treatment of last resort; it may well be that IVF offers the best hope of a healthy pregnancy. In certain instances, the woman may have almost as great a chance of becoming pregnant with IVF as would a fertile woman under natural circumstances. Nevertheless, the couple should understand that IVF is not everything to everyone, and some women will never get pregnant through IVF, no matter how many times they try.

Many infertile couples, having experienced repeated disappointments over the years in their attempts to conceive, have come to our program in desperation. Most had previously tried a variety of unsuccessful procedures: fertility drugs for the woman and/or man, medications to treat various hormonal problems, nonsurgical alternatives such as artificial insemination, and pelvic surgery to repair anatomical defects. A few couples had been advised by their doctor to "take a holiday, just relax and get rid of your stress—and you'll get pregnant. Your problem's just emotional." All these couples looked to IVF as a promising new procedure that might help them conceive after all of their other attempts had failed.

Yet of the more than 500,000 couples in this country for whom in vitro fertilization offers the only real option for a pregnancy, fewer than 20,000 undergo the procedure annually. Clearly, eligible infertile couples in the United States are not even coming close to tapping the potential of IVF. Why is this so?

One reason is because some people still consider IVF to be experimental. However, the evidence proves otherwise—approximately 10,000 IVF babies have already been born worldwide, including about 2000 in the United States. Yet the public as well as many members of the medical profession still know surprisingly little about IVF beyond the often sensational "test-tube baby" media coverage. One new father of an IVF baby explained how misleading that coverage can be:

> People get a distorted idea about IVF when they turn on the TV and see a slide of a test tube with a baby inside. By no means is there either a test tube or a baby at that point. There are just a momentary couple of days when fertilization takes place outside the couple's bodies, and then the embryo is placed in the woman's uterus and begins to grow there. The phrase "test-tube baby" is a convenient handle for the media, but unfortunately it implies a sterility that IVF doesn't have at all.

Unfortunately, consumers find it difficult to get much in-depth information about this exciting new procedure. (In this context, "consumers" refers to both infertile couples and physicians who wish to refer their patients to a particular program.) No credible source provides meaningful information about successful IVF programs in the United States to consumers, and often trying to learn about IVF is like stumbling around in the dark.

Several national organizations, including the Society of Assisted Reproductive Technology (SART, formerly the IVF Special Interest Group of the American Fertility Society) and a number of support groups for infertile couples, provide limited information about IVF and related procedures. The SART was formed in 1988 under the umbrella of the American Fertility Society, which primarily comprises physicians but also includes laboratory personnel, psychologists, nurses, and other paramedical personnel interested in infertility.

The SART will provide a list of IVF programs in the United States; however, it does not recommend or endorse any programs and instead encourages the consumer to contact the programs individually for more information. The list currently does not include data on the programs' success rates or other statistics. (The American Fertility Society, 2131 Magnolia Avenue, Suite 201, Birmingham, AL 35256; telephone 205–251-9764; SART, 205–933-8494.)

The American Fertility Society/SART has taken the first step toward providing consumer-oriented information by compiling a registry of programs that have voluntarily submitted their IVF results. However, we believe that the American Fertility Society probably can take only limited steps in providing information to the consumer because of internal political constraints, including fears by some members that release of statistics on individual programs might lead to creeping regulation. Therefore, it is not likely that the society will be able to provide statistics on a clinic-by-clinic basis in the foreseeable future. Nevertheless, we hope that the registry may be expanded to provide more specific information for consumers.

A number of fertility support groups in the United States provide information about IVF and infertility in general. The largest group is Resolve, Inc., a national, nonprofit organization that offers counseling, referral services, and support to infertile couples (5 Water Street, Arlington, MA 02174; telephone 617–643-2424). Resolve has local chapters throughout the country, and publishes a bimonthly newsletter and other literature about infertility. Resolve and several of the smaller support groups also provide lists of IVF programs, but they are reluctant to recommend specific programs.

Another obstacle to widespread acceptance of IVF is its high cost. In vitro fertilization is relatively expensive ($5000 to $8000 per procedure depending on the program). Some insurance companies currently fund about one-third to one-half of the total cost of IVF [the fertility hormone shots, ultrasound examinations, and the procedure that may be used for egg retrieval (ultrasound or laparoscopy), including operating room and anesthesiologist's fees]. But with few exceptions they still will not pay for laboratory work, the fertilization process, or the embryo transfer.

Because of the financial burden many couples pass up IVF, although it may be the most appropriate treatment for them.

They simply cannot afford it. Several states have passed laws requiring insurance companies to reimburse in total for IVF, and several others are considering similar legislation. Nevertheless, IVF will continue to be beyond the financial reach of most couples in this country until insurance companies adopt equitable reimbursement policies.

We can promise consumers that things are not likely to get better for a long time. Information will be difficult to obtain, and IVF will continue to be expensive. But by researching the IVF situation for themselves, couples will be able to answer these fundamental questions: (1) Are we eligible for IVF? and (2) How do we select the program that will give the best results?

This book has been designed to help answer these critical questions. It describes IVF and some other high-tech procedures; it outlines a variety of emotional, physical, financial, and moral/religious issues; and it highlights points that should be considered when deciding if IVF or some other high-tech procedure is indeed the most appropriate option. We do not offer any judgments on ethics, religion, or morality; these kinds of decisions are private matters that must be resolved by each couple in their own way.

This book is designed to help consumers develop and maintain realistic expectations about IVF. Realistic expectations revolve around the best and the worst possible scenarios, but all infertile couples should prepare themselves for the worst, just in case. But by planning an effective strategy, asking the right questions, and evaluating the answers properly, candidates can determine if they are eligible for IVF, and find the most appropriate program. As a 35-year-old new mother said, doing that homework does pay off:

> I must have spent at least three hours talking with my own physician trying to find out where to go for IVF. It was so frustrating not being able to find anyone who could give me any real answers. Several times I was tempted to go to the IVF clinic nearest us just because it was so convenient. But

thank God I did my homework as thoroughly as I knew how. I must have called up fifteen different programs. I asked a lot of questions about success rates and what it was like to go through their programs, and then I had to sort everything out. I finally found a great program—and now we have a beautiful little girl who is the joy of our lives. I can hardly remember what life had been like without her. It was worth all that effort.

PART I

IVF in Perspective

CHAPTER 1

The Growing
Dilemma of Infertility

It is estimated that there are about 40 million couples of child-bearing age living together in the United States today. Approximately 3.3 million of these couples are infertile.

This estimate is based upon a series of nationwide surveys conducted by the National Center for Health Statistics. The most recent of these surveys was released in 1982; data from a similar study conducted in 1988 will be available in early 1989. The 1982 report, which surveyed cohabiting married couples in which the wives were between 15 to 44 years of age, found that one out of twelve, or 8.5 percent, of the couples were involuntarily infertile. Therefore, the figure of 3.3 million infertile couples was derived by adjusting the percentage slightly upward to allow for unmarried cohabiting couples.

Infertility can be defined as the inability to conceive after one full year of normal, regular heterosexual intercourse without the use of any contraception. The odds that a woman will get pregnant without medical assistance when she has failed to do so after a year or two of unprotected intercourse are abysmally low.

Only couples who have experienced the problem of infertility can truly understand its devastating emotional and physical impact. As one woman, who had been trying unsuccessfully to become pregnant for many years, explained:

> It has been two years since I learned the reason I wasn't getting pregnant was because my fallopian tubes were blocked. It is incredible to think that I have had more physical assault on my body in the last two years than in the rest of my thirty years combined. I underwent it voluntarily, too, because I wanted to correct the problem and have a child. Yet, all the surgeries, the tests, and the medications seemed relatively minor compared to the emotional burden I put on myself.
>
> After my first surgery, when my physician said it was okay to try to become pregnant, I don't think there was ever a day, or perhaps an hour, that I didn't think about conceiving. It was always there—when I would see a child in the grocery store; when my friends would gripe about their kids; when I was on day 1, or day 14, and every other day of my menstrual cycle; and whenever my husband and I made love. Was I ever going to get pregnant? I had conflicting fantasies of what I would be like as a mother, or what I would be like as a 60-year-old woman who had never had children. I could never get it out of my mind.

One study of infertile couples illustrates the pervasive impacts of infertility. When asked what they considered to be the primary problem in their lives, almost 80 percent of the couples replied that it was their inability to conceive. Most of the remaining 20 percent ranked infertility as their second most perplexing problem, after financial difficulties. The remaining fraction of respondents rated infertility a close third after financial problems and marital strife.

One newly pregnant woman, who had just completed her second IVF treatment cycle, summed up the emotional impact of infertility in this way:

> You really can't understand what it's like to be infertile unless you are infertile yourself and have experienced what

we've gone through. You can sympathize, but you can't empathize with us.

The traditional options available to infertile couples who want a baby have included counseling, surgery to repair anatomical damage, the use of fertility drugs to enhance ovulation and sperm function, and insemination of the woman with her partner's or a donor's sperm. Most authorities would agree that these methods are effective for approximately 70 to 85 percent of all infertile couples.

For the remaining 15 to 30 percent, or about 500,000 couples annually in the United States, the only recourse is IVF—yet only about 20,000 IVF procedures were performed in 1988.

Why the Number of Infertile Couples in the United States Is Increasing Every Year

According to the National Center for Health Statistics the rate of involuntary infertility discussed at the beginning of this chapter has remained constant at about 8.5 percent since 1965, an increase from the early 1950s through 1964, when it is thought approximately 7 to 8 percent of all couples were unable to conceive. Although the rate of infertility has not changed since the mid-1960s, the number of infertile couples has increased every year in accordance with population growth in the United States. The following factors contribute to this trend.

Venereal Diseases Are Epidemic in the United States

Once brought largely under control because of the discovery and availability of proper medication, the incidence of venereal diseases that damage reproductive systems is again rising. One of the major causes of this is the increased availability of effective birth control methods, which has undoubtedly contributed to a more permissive approach toward sexual activity. Consequently, both men and women often have relatively large numbers of sexual partners. The unfortunate result has been a significant increase in sexually transmitted diseases.

Venereal diseases such as *gonorrhea* are rampant in the United States. Gonorrhea lodges in the woman's fallopian tubes and often results in a severe illness. Unfortunately, in many cases gonorrhea causes so little physical discomfort that women frequently do not bother to seek treatment. But even a minor gonorrheal infection can damage the fallopian tubes, and many women only find out they have had gonorrhea when they investigate the cause of their infertility. In contrast, gonorrhea in men almost invariably produces sudden, painful symptoms that usually prompt an immediate visit to the doctor. For this reason, men are less likely to be infertile due to gonorrhea than women.

The cure of sexually transmitted diseases is complicated by the emergence of new strains of gonorrhea and other venereal diseases that resist traditional treatment. These bacteria can be treated only by new and expensive antibiotics that often are not readily available.

Chlamydia, another infection that blocks the fallopian tubes, is as prevalent today as gonorrhea. Chlamydia is very difficult to diagnose and culture, and it only responds well to specific antibiotics.

Finally, *syphilis* is becoming widespread again in the United States. Syphilis can be easily cured in the early stages, but in the later stages, its spread can be halted, but its effects cannot be reversed.

The "Biological Clock" Keeps Ticking

Many women today choose to delay beginning a family until they are at least 30 in order to establish their careers or to be sure they and their partners "can afford it." However, there is sometimes a price to pay for having children later on. For example, some disorders that produce infertility tend to appear during the second half of a woman's reproductive life-span. Accordingly, a woman who decides to have children after 35 might find she is infertile because of hormonal problems, a pelvic disease such as endometriosis, or the development of benign fibroid tumors of the uterus. In addition, the ability to ovulate and concurrently generate a hormonal environment that can adequately support a pregnancy becomes increasingly difficult as a woman gets older. Thus, many women who plan to become pregnant later in their reproductive lives find themselves unable to do so.

Medications and "Recreational Drugs" Are Taking Their Toll

Alcohol, cigarettes, marijuana, cocaine, and other psychotropic drugs can significantly reduce both male and female fertility because they alter the structure of eggs and sperm. However, these substances can potentially have a far more severe and long-lasting effect on the woman than the man. Because a woman is born with a lifetime quota of eggs already inside her ovaries, unwise use of medications and drugs can damage all the eggs her body will ever produce. In contrast, a man generates a completely new supply of sperm approximately every three months, so damaged sperm are replaced in a short time (see Chapter 2).

Due to the natural population growth in the United States, the number of couples whose last option for pregnancy is one of the new high-tech procedures is skyrocketing. Fortunately, recent advances in the evolution of high-tech methods to evaluate and treat infertility offer the hope of pregnancy to couples who never had any hope until now. In vitro fertilization is just one of these promising procedures, but in many cases it offers the best hope for success.

CHAPTER 2

The Anatomy and Physiology of Reproduction

In vitro fertilization can be viewed as an extension of the normal human reproductive process. In vitro fertilization merely bypasses many of the anatomical or physiological causes of infertility by substituting IVF techniques for some of the processes that occur naturally in the body. In order to understand both natural conception and IVF, therefore, one must first be familiar with human reproductive anatomy and the process of reproduction.

The Female Reproductive Tract

The female reproductive tract consists of the vulva, vagina, cervix, uterus, fallopian tubes, and ovaries.

The external portion of the female reproductive tract is known as the *vulva*. The vulva includes the inner and outer lips, or *labia*. The hair-covered outer labia are called the *labia majora* (major lips). The *labia minora,* small inner lips partially hidden by the labia majora, are remnants of tissue whose embryologic counterpart in the male develops into the scrotum.

The *clitoris,* a small organ at the junction of the labia minora in the front of the vulva, is the embryologic counterpart of the male penis. The clitoris undergoes erection during erotic stimulation and plays an important role in orgasm.

The area between the labia minora and the anus is called the *perineum.* It is formed by the outer portion of the fibro-

THE EXTERNAL GENITAL ORGANS OF THE FEMALE

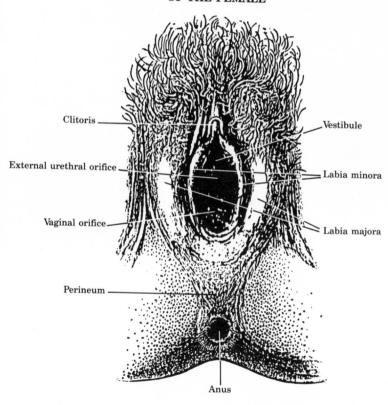

Clitoris

Vestibule

External urethral orifice

Labia minora

Vaginal orifice

Labia majora

Perineum

Anus

FIGURE 2-1

THE FEMALE PELVIC ORGANS
(SIDE VIEW)

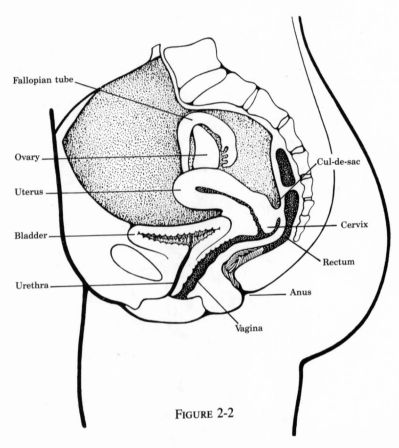

Fallopian tube

Ovary

Uterus

Bladder

Urethra

Cul-de-sac

Cervix

Rectum

Anus

Vagina

FIGURE 2-2

muscular wall and skin that separate the *anus* and *rectum* from the vagina and vulva.

The *vagina,* a narrow passage about 3½ to 4 inches long and about 1 inch wide, spans the area between the vulva and cervix. It opens outward through the cleft between the labia minora, or *vestibule.* The vagina's elastic tissue, muscle, and skin have enormous ability to stretch so as to accommodate the penis during the sex act and the passage of a baby at birth. The vagina is actually a potential space; it is only a real space

THE FEMALE PELVIC ORGANS
(FRONT VIEW)

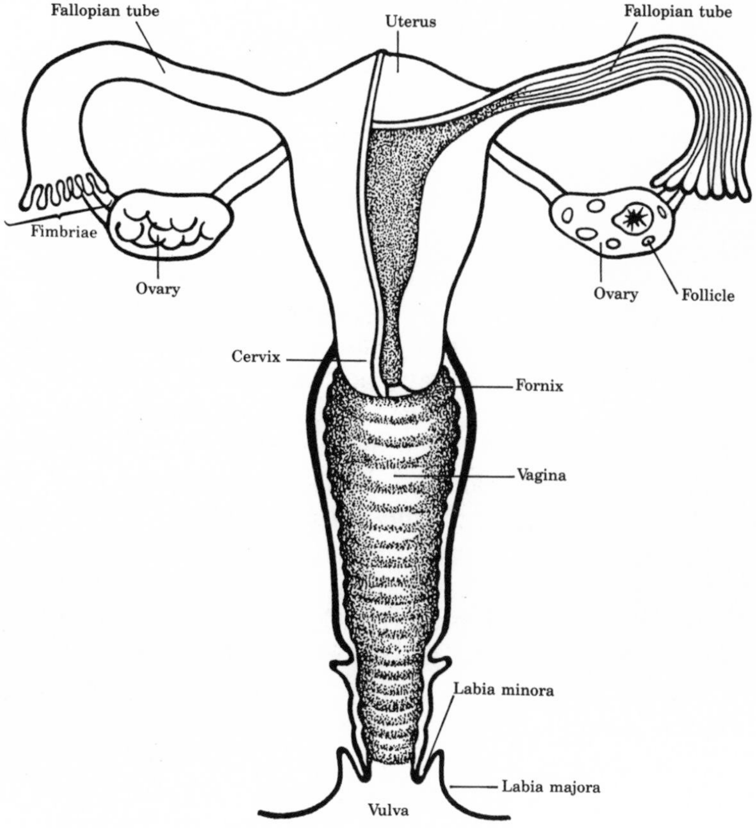

Fallopian tube · Uterus · Fallopian tube · Fimbriae · Ovary · Ovary · Follicle · Cervix · Fornix · Vagina · Labia minora · Labia majora · Vulva

FIGURE 2-3

when the penis enters it or during childbirth. At other times, the vaginal walls are collapsed against one another; a cross-section of a relaxed vagina would resemble the letter H. At the front of the vagina lie the *bladder* and *urethra* (outlet from the bladder), and at the back is the rectum.

The *cervix*, which is the lowermost part of the uterus, protrudes like a bottleneck into the upper vagina. As Figure 2-3 illustrates, a *fornix,* or deep recess, is created around the area where the cervix extends into the vagina. The area of the abdominal cavity behind the uterus is known as the *cul-de-sac.* The cervix opens into the uterus through a narrow canal, the lining of which contains glands that produce cervical mucus (the important role that cervical mucus plays in the reproductive process will be explained later). The cervix is particularly vulnerable to infections and other diseases such as cancer.

The *uterus,* which consists of strong muscle fibers, is able to grow and stretch from its normal size resembling a pear to accommodate a full-term pregnancy. The valve-like transition between the cervix and uterine cavity enables a baby to grow within the uterus without prematurely dilating the cervix and thereby endangering the pregnancy through miscarriage or premature birth. The lining of the uterus, which nurtures and supports the developing embryo, is known as the *endometrium.*

The *fallopian tubes* are two narrow 4-inch-long structures that lead from either side of the uterus to the ovaries. At the end of the fallopian tubes are finger-like protrusions known as *fimbriae.*

The *ovaries* are two almond-like structures that are attached to each side of the pelvis adjacent to the fimbriae. The ovaries both release *eggs* and discharge certain hormones into the bloodstream. The process of releasing the egg or eggs is called *ovulation.*

These eggs—each about the size of a grain of sand—are the largest cells in the human body. They are also known as *ova,* or *oocytes.* A woman is born with her lifetime supply of eggs inside her ovaries, and each month the ovaries select a number of these eggs for maturation. However, only one egg, and sometimes two, actually reach the stage where they are mature enough to be released and possibly fertilized. Eggs that do not mature are absorbed by the ovaries after ovulation.

Although a female baby starts off with about 7 million eggs when she is inside her mother's womb, her ovaries contain only about 700,000 eggs by the time she reaches puberty. A woman uses about 300,000 of these eggs during the approximately 400 ovulations that occur during her reproductive lifespan.

Eggs mature in blister-like structures known as *follicles* that project from the surface of the ovaries. At ovulation, the egg is not simply expelled into the abdominal cavity. Instead, the fimbriae at the end of the fallopian tubes gently vacuum the surface of the ovaries to retrieve the egg and direct it through the fallopian tube for possible fertilization.

The human egg is similar in structure to the eggs of many other species, including the chicken. In the center of the human egg is the *nucleus,* which bears the chromosomes. The surrounding *ooplasm,* contains *microorganelles,* which are cellular factories that produce energy for the egg. The ooplasm also contains nurturing material that supports the embryo during its early stages after fertilization, enabling it to grow before becoming attached to an external source of nourishment. Surrounding the ooplasm and nuclear material is the *perivitelline membrane,* which separates the internal matter from the *zona pellucida.* The zona pellucida is analogous to the shell of a chicken egg, and the perivitelline membrane corresponds to the membrane inside the eggshell. The human egg, unlike the chicken egg, also contains a group of cells arranged in a sunburst effect around the zona pellucida, known as the *cumulus mass,* or *corona radiata.* (The critical role each of these structures plays in the fertilization process is explained later in this chapter under "How Fertilization Occurs.")

The Male Reproductive Tract

The male sex organs comprise the *penis* and two *testicles,* or *testes,* which are located in a pouch called the *scrotum.* The testicles (male counterparts of the woman's ovaries) produce *spermatozoa,* or *sperm.*

In contrast to the woman, who is born with a lifetime quota of eggs, the man's testicles generate a new complement of sperm approximately every 100 days. The sperm begin to mature in the testicles and continue to develop as they travel through a long, thin coiled tubular system in the scrotum called the *epididymis*. The epididymis is connected to a straight, thicker tube called the *vas deferens*. Just before the vas deferens enters the penis it joins the *urethra*, which originates in the bladder and allows the passage of urine from the bladder through the penis. Sperm are transported through this system by muscular contractions.

Several glands, including the *seminal vesicles* and the *prostate gland*, are located along this tract. These glands release a

A HUMAN EGG

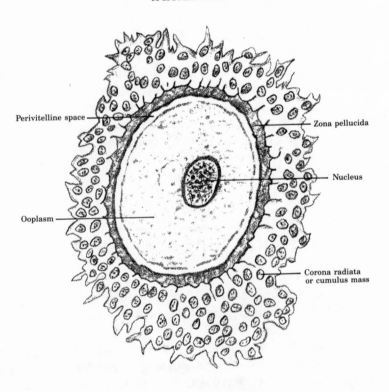

FIGURE 2-4

large amount of milky secretions that nurture and promote the survival of the sperm. The combination of sperm and milky fluid that is ejaculated during erotic experiences is known as *semen*. (Semen and urine are not discharged simultaneously through the urethra. Urine is prevented from mixing with semen in the urethra because the bladder-urethra opening constricts during ejaculation; similarly, closure of the vas deferens-urethra juncture prevents passage of semen during urination. In certain cases, removal of a diseased prostate gland may compromise this separation effect and cause the man to ejaculate backward into the bladder rather than outward through the penis; this is known as *retrograde ejaculation*. This condition may cause infertility, but it can be treated by inseminating the woman with sperm separated from urine the man would pass immediately following orgasm.)

Microscopically, sperm resemble tadpoles. Each sperm consists of a head, whose *nucleus* contains the hereditary or genetic material arrayed on chromosomes, a midsection that provides energy, and a tail that propels the sperm along the male reproductive system and through the woman's reproductive tract. The top of the head is covered by the *acrosome*, a protective structure containing enzymes that enable the sperm to penetrate the egg; and the surface of the acrosome is enveloped by the *plasma membrane*. (The function of the acrosome and plasma membrane will be explained under "How Fertilization Occurs" later in this chapter.)

How the Genetic Blueprint Is Drawn

Each cell in a human being (except for the *gametes*, or eggs and sperm) contains forty-six chromosomes, which are bound together into twenty-three pairs. Chromosomes contain hun-

THE MALE REPRODUCTIVE SYSTEM

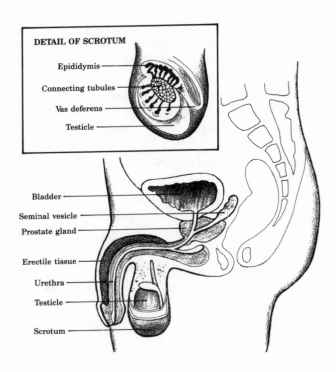

DETAIL OF SCROTUM

Epididymis

Connecting tubules

Vas deferens

Testicle

Bladder

Seminal vesicle

Prostate gland

Erectile tissue

Urethra

Testicle

Scrotum

FIGURE 2-5

THE MATURE SPERM

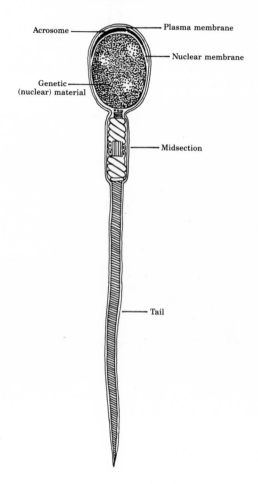

FIGURE 2-6

dreds of thousands of genes, each of which transmits the hereditary messages of the man or woman.

If a sperm containing forty-six chromosomes were to fertilize an egg that also contains forty-six chromosomes, it is obvious that the two gametes would produce a *zygote* containing double the proper number of chromosomes. (A fertilized egg is called a zygote until it begins to divide; from initial cell division through the first eight weeks of gestation it is known as an *embryo;* and from the ninth week of gestation until delivery, the embryo is called a *fetus.*) Therefore, nature has decreed that the number of chromosomes in both the sperm and the egg be reduced by half. This reduction-division, which occurs immediately prior to and during fertilization, is referred to as *meiosis* (see Figure 2-7).

Consequently, a newly fertilized zygote also contains forty-six chromosomes. All that has been exchanged is the chromosomal material, including the genes. The intermingling of genetic material from both the woman and man results in a new individual with a new blueprint.

When the cells of the zygote begin to divide, and continue to divide over and over, they perpetuate the same number of chromosomes that occurred in the zygote. Thus, every new cell has twenty-three identical pairs of chromosomes (forty-six total) in its own new image. Such division for the purpose of replicating cells identically is called *mitosis.* The growth and development of all tissues—with the exception, of course, of the gametes—is done by mitosis.

Obviously, such a sensitive, intricate mechanism can and often does go wrong. Because this process malfunctions so often, nature has to have a way of selecting out its mistakes and discarding them. This will be discussed later in this chapter under "Miscarriage in Early Pregnancy."

HOW MEIOSIS PREPARES THE GAMETES
FOR FERTILIZATION

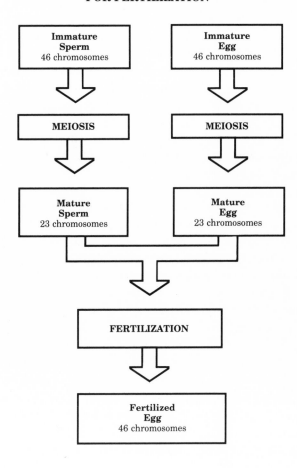

FIGURE 2-7

The Process of Fertilization

Fertilization is a complex process that must be accomplished within a strict time frame. Theoretically, a man is always fertile, but a woman's egg can only be fertilized within a specific 12- to 24-hour period shortly after ovulation. Therefore, there is only a "window of opportunity" between 24 to 48 hours each month when intercourse can be expected to result in fertilization. Timing is critical if the egg and sperm are to survive the journey through the woman's reproductive tract, unite, become fertilized, and result in the embryo implanting successfully into the uterine wall.

The man deposits between 100 and 200 million sperm into the woman's vagina with each ejaculation of semen. During normal intercourse, or even after the woman has been artificially inseminated, much of the semen pools in the posterior fornix behind the protruding cervix. Because the cervix usually points partially backward into the posterior fornix, the cervix is usually immersed in the pool of ejaculated semen. This immersion helps direct the sperm through the cervix and into the reproductive tract.

The journey from the fornix to the fallopian tubes is hazardous and unbelievably taxing for the tiny sperm. Only a small fraction of exceptionally strong, healthy sperm out of several million that were deposited in the fornix will survive that 24- to 48-hour journey. Many are killed by a hostile environment in the vagina or cervix, and others simply do not survive the long swim. Muscular contractions in the fallopian tubes help the successful sperm reach the egg, and the same contractions propel the fertilized egg or embryo back through the fallopian tube to the uterus.

How Fertilization Occurs

The process whereby sperm are prepared to fertilize an egg is known as *capacitation,* and takes place in two stages. First, as a sperm passes through the woman's reproductive tract its acrosome fuses with the plasma membrane, slowly releasing the enzymes within the acrosome. Second, a sperm, with its acrosome now exposed, attacks the cumulus-zona complex of the egg; the head of the sperm fuses with the zona pellucida and then penetrates the egg. The process whereby a sperm fuses with the zona, the second stage of capacitation, is called the *acrosome reaction.*

Capacitation takes place in the mucus secretions of the cervical canal, and continues in the uterus and fallopian tubes. It is believed that the passage of sperm through the cervical mucus around the time of ovulation promotes the necessary physical, chemical, and structural changes in the plasma membrane to facilitate release of acrosomal enzymes. (Because only sperm that have undergone capacitation are able to fertilize an egg, in IVF therapy the first stage of capacitation must be replicated in the laboratory prior to IVF if fertilization is to occur in the petri dish.)

After the acrosome reaction has taken place, a sperm completes the fertilization process by burrowing through the zona pellucida (the egg's shell-like covering) and ooplasm to the nuclear material. The sperm sheds its body and tail upon penetration, and only the head (containing the genetic material) actually enters the egg. Figure 2-8 illustrates the following steps in the capacitation-fertilization process: Phase 1: The plasma membrane fuses with the acrosome as the sperm pass into the reproductive tract to reach the egg, thus initiating capacitation. Phase 2a: The acrosomal enzymes are released and penetrate the cumulus mass (corona radiata) cells of the egg. Phase 2b: The acrosome fuses with the zona pellucida, thus completing capacitation. Phase 3: The sperm burrows through the zona pellucida into the ooplasm of the egg.

The moment a sperm penetrates the egg's zona pellucida, a reaction in the egg fuses the zona and the perivitelline membrane into an impermeable shield that prevents other sperm from entering. The entry of more than one sperm into a fertilized egg (called *polyspermia*) causes the resulting embryo to die.

When fertilization occurs, the egg starts dividing within the

THE CAPACITATION-FERTILIZATION PROCESS

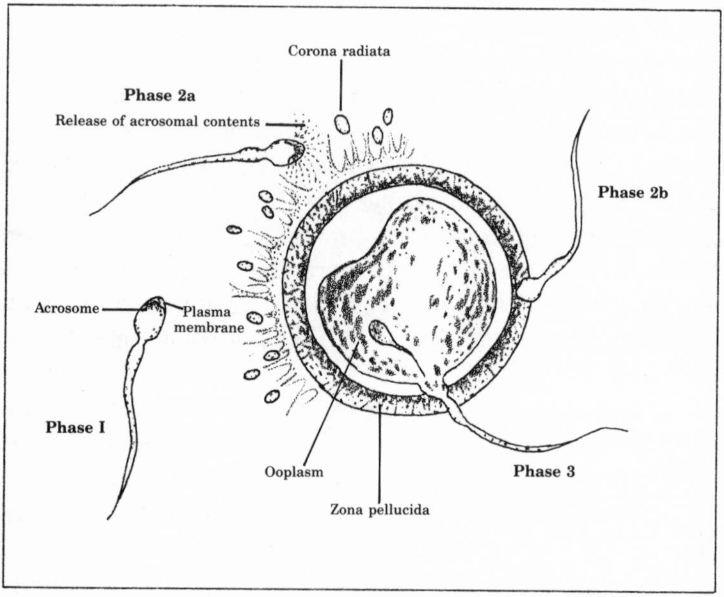

FIGURE 2-8

zona covering, drawing its metabolic supplies from the ooplasm within the egg. Propelled by contractions of the fallopian tube, the dividing embryo begins its three- or four-day journey back to the uterus and continues to divide after it reaches the uterus. (The fertilization process occurs near the middle of the fallopian tube—not in the uterus.) About twodays after reaching the uterus, when the embryo has divided into about thirty cells, it bursts through the zona and implants itself into the endometrium. A portion of the growing embryo soon makes contact with the mother's circulatory system, and becomes the earliest form of the placenta from which the baby will receive its nourishment (see Figure 2-9).

If an embryo implants anywhere but the uterus it is referred to as an *ectopic pregnancy*. In most cases an ectopic pregnancy is due to embryonic implantation in the fallopian tube; this occurs about once in every 200 pregnancies. Isolated cases of implantation in the reproductive tract, such as on the ovary or elsewhere in the abdominal cavity, have been reported; in rare instances such ectopic pregnancies have been known to develop to full term, but the baby invariably will not survive. Figure 2-9 follows the progress of an egg as it is ovulated from the follicle, becomes fertilized in the fallopian tube, and implants into the endometrium of the uterus. The dotted line plots the days that normally elapse as: (a) ovulation occurs (and meiosis takes place prior to and during fertilization); (b) the fertilized egg, which has

**TIME LINE FOR OVULATION,
FERTILIZATION, AND
IMPLANTATION**

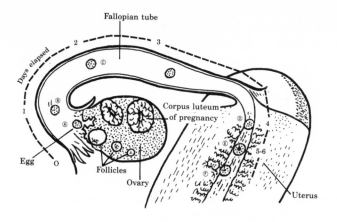

FIGURE 2-9

not yet divided, is now known as a *zygote;* (c) the egg begins to divide and is now known as an *embryo;* at this point each *blasto-mere,* or cell, within the embryo is capable of developing into an identical embryo; (d) the embryo develops into a mulberry-like structure known as a *morulla;* (e) a cavity develops within the embryo, which has reached the *blastocyst* stage; (f) the process of *gastrulation* begins (cells now are dedicated to the development of specific embryonic layers that subsequently will form specific organs and structures; individual cells are no longer capable of developing into embryos).

The Role of the Cervical Mucus

At ovulation, the physical-chemical properties of the cervical mucus nurture the sperm as they pass through it, favoring their quick passage and therefore capacitation as well. This is be-cause hormonal changes around the time of ovulation ensure that the microfibrilles, or *myceles,* of the cervical mucus are arranged in a parallel manner. The sperm must then swim be-tween the myceles in order to reach the uterus and finally the fallopian tubes. In addition, the cervical mucus becomes wa-tery, and the amount produced (some of which may be dis-charged) increases significantly.

At other times during the menstrual cycle the hormonal en-vironment alters the arrangement of the myceles in the cervical mucus to form a barrier to the passage of sperm. During this time the mucus is thick, thus preventing the sperm from passing through the cervix.

The *Billings Method* of contraception is based on this phe-nomenon. A woman using the Billings Method predicts when she is likely to be ovulating by evaluating whether her cervical mucus is thick or watery. Because pregnancy can only occur around the time of ovulation, it is accordingly possible for her to identify the so-called "safe period" when she is unlikely to conceive following unprotected intercourse.

Hormones Prepare the Body for Conception

Pregnancy, of course, begins with the fusion of two gametes—the female egg and the male sperm—but the preparations for conception begin long before fertilization occurs. Puberty in both the man and woman sets the stage for a biorhythmical hormonal orchestration that becomes more and more fine-tuned over the ensuing decade. It begins with the formation and release of hormones into the bloodstream, and the bodies of both sexes rely on a complex feedback mechanism to measure the existing hormonal level and determine when additional hormones should be released.

The *hypothalamus* (a small area in the midportion of the brain) and the *pituitary gland* (a small, grape-like structure that hangs from the base of the brain by a thin stalk) together regulate the formation and release of hormones. The hypothalamus, through its sensors, or "receptors," constantly monitors female and male hormonal concentrations in the bloodstream and responds by regulating the release of small protein-like "messenger hormones" to the pituitary gland. These messenger hormones are known as *gonadotropin-releasing hormones,* or *GnRH* (see Figure 2-10).

In response to the messenger hormones from the hypothalamus, the pituitary gland determines the exact amount of hormones that it in turn will release to stimulate the *gonads* (ovaries in the woman and testicles in the man). These hormones, which are called *gonadotropins,* are *FSH (follicle-stimulating hormones)* and *LH (luteinizing hormones).* The hypothalamus closes the feedback circle by measuring the level of hormones produced by the gonads while at the same time monitoring the release of LH and FSH by the pituitary gland.

This "push-pull" interplay of messages and responses produces the cyclical hormonal environment in the woman that is designed solely to promote pregnancy. A "push-pull" mech-

THE INTERRELATIONSHIP OF HORMONES
IN THE WOMAN

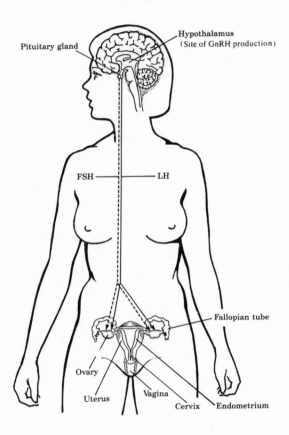

FIGURE 2-10

anism also occurs in the man with regard to the release of testosterone. Similar feedback mechanisms regulate other hormonal responses in mammals, such as the functioning of the thyroid and adrenal glands.

There are two primary sex hormones in the female, *estrogen* and *progesterone;* in the male only one, *testosterone.* The pituitary gland releases identical hormones—FSH and LH—to the gonads of both the woman (the ovaries) and the man (testicles), but the female and male gonads respond differently to these hormones. The level of female hormones fluctuates approximately monthly throughout the menstrual cycle while male hormone production remains relatively constant.

In men, FSH and LH trigger the production of *testosterone* and influence the production and maturation of sperm. (The mechanism of male hormone production is not relevant to a proper understanding of IVF and will not be discussed in detail here.)

In women, extraneous factors as well as the level of circulating hormones and gonadotropins may influence the body's feedback mechanism. For example, the hypothalamus is also influenced by stress, pain, environmental changes, diseases in the woman's body, birth control pills, and many forms of medication, including tranquilizers and blood-pressure medication.

The best way to understand this cyclical hormonal process is to trace the woman's hormonal pattern throughout a menstrual cycle. (For practical purposes, the menstrual cycle will be considered to begin on the first day of menstruation. The following illustration is based on a 28-day menstrual cycle. However, it is important to remember that some women have menstrual cycles of other than 28 days. In such cases, although the cyclic phases and ovulation occur in the manner described below, their length and timing vary according to the number of days in that particular cycle. For example, a woman with a cycle of 35 days is not likely to ovulate on day 14.)

The First Half of the Cycle
(the Follicular/Proliferative Phase)

During the first two weeks of the menstrual cycle the body prepares for ovulation (release of one or more eggs from the ovary). During this two-week period, until ovulation, the lining of the uterus (endometrium) thickens or proliferates significantly and becomes very glandular under the influence of rising blood estrogen levels. This phase is accordingly often referred to as the *proliferative phase* of the cycle; and because this proliferation of the endometrium occurs at the same time as the development of the ovarian follicle or follicles, it is often also known as the *follicular phase*. From just prior to the scheduled menstrual period until the middle of that cycle, the pituitary gland releases the gonadotropin FSH in ever-increasing amounts. This stimulates the production of the hormone estrogen by the ovaries.

The release of FSH and subsequent production of estrogen precipitates the formation of follicles on the ovaries and the selection of eggs (usually one per follicle) to mature during that cycle. As many as six to eight or even more follicles begin to develop under the stimulation of FSH from the pituitary gland, but in the natural cycle only one and sometimes two follicles progress to ovulation. The eggs that do not mature are absorbed into the ovary. This explains why so many eggs are lost during the reproductive life span, although a woman usually ovulates only one, sometimes two, and very rarely three in any particular menstrual cycle.

When a woman has used up most of her lifetime quota and is left with less than a critical number of eggs, she begins to enter a phase of hormonal change known as the *climacteric*. The climacteric is associated with a loss of fertility, hot flashes, mood changes, and usually a reevaluation of self-worth. It ultimately culminates with the total cessation of menstruation between the ages of 40 to 55, a process called the *menopause*. After menopause, the ovaries still produce hormones; but they are then released in a constant rather than a cyclical manner.

Responding (usually at the middle of the menstrual cycle) to the rising estrogen levels in the bloodstream of hormonally normal young women, the hypothalamus releases a surge of gonadotropin-releasing hormone (GnRH) when the estrogen reaches a critical level. This rush in GnRH production prompts the pituitary gland to produce a surge of LH, which had only been released in very low, erratic concentrations until this point. It is the sudden surge in LH that actually triggers ovulation.

Ovulation

At ovulation, a muscle connecting the ovary with the end of the fallopian tube contracts, bringing the fimbriae closer to the follicle containing the egg. The fimbriae then gently vacuum and massage the follicle until the egg, which by this time is protruding from the follicle, is extruded. The fimbriae receive the egg and direct it into a fallopian tube, where muscular contractions transport it toward the uterus.

The follicle collapses once the egg has been extruded, and is transformed biochemically and hormonally. It takes on a yellowish color and is then referred to as the "yellow body," or *corpus luteum* in Latin.

The endometrium develops throughout the cycle in preparation for receiving an embryo, and by the time ovulation occurs it is about three times as thick as it was immediately after menstruation.

The Second Half of the Cycle (the Secretory/Luteal Phase)

Once the corpus luteum forms, the ovary begins to secrete the hormone progesterone as well as estrogen; and the levels of progesterone begin to rise very rapidly. The progesterone converts the proliferated, glandular endometrium to a juicy structure capable of secreting a substance that will sustain an embryo, hence the term *secretory phase of the menstrual cycle*. The term *luteal*

THE STAGES OF FOLLICULAR DEVELOPMENT
IN THE OVARY

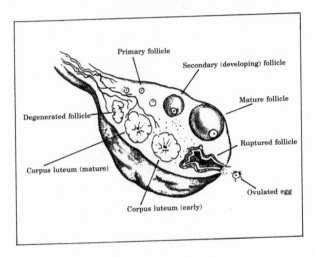

FIGURE 2-11

phase describes the stage during which the corpus luteum produces the progesterone that enhances the secretory environment in the uterus.

The corpus luteum, through the production of both estrogen and progesterone, supports the survival of the secretory endometrium through the second half of the menstrual cycle. The lifespan of the corpus luteum is about 12 to 14 days if fertilization and implantation of the embryo into the lining of the uterus do not occur. During that period the endometrium is sustained by the estrogen and progesterone produced by the corpus luteum. Once the corpus luteum begins to die, the hormonal support for the lining of the uterus is lost, and two-thirds of the endometrium comes away (often with the unfertilized egg or unimplanted embryo) in the form of *menstruation*. (Figure 2-12 illustrates the relationship of hormone production to follicular and endometrial development throughout the menstrual cycle.)

Should the woman become pregnant, the hormone produced by the implanting embryo and the developing placenta (*human chorionic gonadotropin,* or hCG, which has a similar effect on the corpus luteum to LH) prolongs the survival of the corpus luteum beyond its normal 12- to 14-day lifespan. The corpus luteum, in turn, continues to produce the hormones estrogen and

THE RELATIONSHIP OF HORMONE PRODUCTION
TO FOLLICULAR AND ENDOMETRIAL DEVELOPMENT

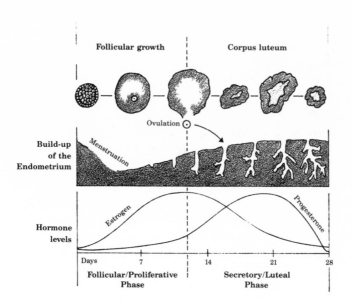

FIGURE 2-12

progesterone to maintain the secretory environment of the endometrium, which nurtures the growth of the embryo before it makes contact with the blood system of the mother. Because the corpus luteum continues to exist and produces hormones that nurture the endometrium, the woman will miss her next menstrual period and should then suspect that she is pregnant.

The *placenta* begins to form as the developing embryo establishes a connection with the mother's system. The placenta is both the lifeline between the mother's and baby's blood systems as well as the factory that nourishes the baby as pregnancy advances. Because it is capable of producing estrogen and progesterone, the placenta soon supplants the need for hormone production by the corpus luteum and supports the endometrium's survival itself after the sixtieth to seventieth day following the last menstrual period. It has been proved that a pregnancy would continue after the seventieth or eightieth day even if both ovaries were removed because the placental hormones themselves are by then fully capable of sustaining the pregnancy without the hormones produced by the corpus luteum.

After ovulation the production of both LH and FSH declines significantly. If pregnancy does not occur, the hypothalamus begins to secrete more gonadotropin-releasing hormone when the corpus luteum begins to die, thus initiating the next menstrual cycle. The same procedure is repeated over and over, with each hormonal cycle setting up the following one, much as each wave in the ocean sets up and determines the character and magnitude of the following wave. It is an indication of nature's ability to maintain biorhythms in a bewildering but organized fashion.

Miscarriage in Early Pregnancy

Only about one out of every three embryos implants in the uterus long enough to delay the menstrual period. In other words, in two out of every three pregnancies the woman is not even aware that she has conceived.

Even when a pregnancy has been confirmed by a doctor, there is still a 16 to 20 percent chance of *miscarriage* (expelling of the products of conception after the death of the embryo/fetus) during the first three months. In most cases the reason for this remains unapparent. But in those situations where a reason is known, the vast majority of miscarriages are attributed to either an abnormality in the developing offspring or hormonal insufficiency.

The use of sophisticated ultrasound techniques to confirm and monitor pregnancies has led to awareness of the phenomenon that not all embryos that implant in the uterus necessarily develop further. In some cases of confirmed multiple pregnancies, one (or more) of the implanted embryos are absorbed by the body or miscarried and passed through the vagina, thus reducing the number of surviving embryos. This spontaneous reduction in the number of pregnancies appears to be far more common than previously believed, even in those multiple pregnancies occurring without the use of fertility drugs.

An Abnormal Embryo

Early miscarriages usually occur because the embryo is abnormal. Preventing implantation is nature's way of protecting the species from an inordinate number of abnormal offspring. These early miscarriages, which mostly occur even before the woman misses her period, are called *spontaneous menstrual abortions*.

The vast majority of such cases are the consequence of abnormal development in the mixing and replicating of the hereditary blueprint. It has been shown that 60 percent of early pregnancy losses are attributable to a breakdown in the process of early mitosis and meiosis.

As a result of the natural aging process, meiosis and mitosis are far less likely to occur without problems because an older woman's eggs are not able to divide or be fertilized as perfectly as those of a younger woman. This is why the babies of older women are more prone to Down's syndrome and other chromosome abnormalities.

It is probable that fewer meiotic and mitotic problems occur after IVF than after natural conception. This is because in IVF therapy the uterus does not receive the early embryo by the usual route at the hormonally right time, thus making it even more difficult for imperfect embryos, which are often aborted in the natural setting due to their flawed nature, to implant and survive.

Hormonal Insufficiency

In about 10 to 15 percent of all pregnancies, the embryo fails to implant because the amounts of hormones produced and the timing of their release were not perfectly synchronized. Such miscarriages, which may occur even if the embryo is perfect in every way, are attributed to *hormonal insufficiency*. This condition is caused by inadequate production of estrogen and/or progesterone during the menstrual cycle.

If hormonal insufficiency occurs because of abnormal hormonal production of estrogen during the follicular phase of the menstrual cycle, it is known as a *follicular phase insufficiency*. If attributable to inadequate production of hormones by the corpus luteum during the second phase of the cycle, it is referred to as a *luteal phase insufficiency*. Miscarriages due to follicular or luteal phase insufficiency may be associated with ovulation that occurs at the wrong time (either too late or too early), the production of inadequate amounts of hormones, or an endometrium that responds inappropriately to a combination of these factors.

Hormonal insufficiency may be perpetuated into early pregnancy, when the embryo is dependent upon the survival of the corpus luteum before the placenta develops. Obviously, if implantation is imperfect because of improper hormonal stimulation, then *placentation* (the attachment of the placenta to the uterine wall) might also be defective. Poor placental attachment might prevent the baby from getting the proper nutrition; as a result, the baby might grow improperly, and might be born too small or too early.

A pregnancy compromised by hormonal insufficiency may delay the onset of the anticipated menstrual period but then result in early miscarriage because of the inadequate hormonal environment. It is sometimes possible, however, to administer certain hormones in early pregnancy to sustain an embryo that otherwise would be lost.

Additional causes of miscarriage include thyroid and other hormonal irregularities, and kidney problems. In addition to causing miscarriage, it is believed that the abuse and misuse of recreational narcotics, psychotropic drugs, and alcohol and nicotine during the first three months of pregnancy, when cell and organ differentiation is taking place, might significantly increase the incidence of birth defects and inhibit fetal growth and development.

It is the start in life that counts, and in most cases nature catches its mistakes. Nature's high rate of embryo wastage and early miscarriage when conception occurs naturally may come as a surprise to many couples. However, it should provide a helpful perspective for couples who are considering comparable pregnancy rates offered by IVF and other options.

CHAPTER 3

Natural Conception and IVF: Two Pathways to Pregnancy

As Chapter 2 explained, natural conception occurs when the woman ovulates one or more healthy, mature eggs that unite with the man's normal, healthy, mature sperm. In order for conception to take place, both egg and sperm must travel unimpeded through the reproductive tract and must be fertilized in a supportive hormonal environment. Until recently, pregnancy was not possible for couples who could not fulfill both sides of the transport = viability equation. In vitro fertilization often solves this equation by bridging anatomical or physiologic disorders that until now have made pregnancy only an elusive dream for many couples (see next section, "Organic and Physiologic Problems That May Prevent Couples from Conceiving Naturally").

The information below presents the criteria a couple must meet in order for pregnancy to occur naturally:

Criteria Required for Natural Conception

1. Ovulation of a mature, healthy egg or eggs at the appropriate time, in association with the proper hormonal environment.

2. Production of strong, healthy, mature sperm that are deposited in or adjacent to the woman's cervical canal around the time of ovulation.

3. A physical-chemical environment that facilitates capacitation of the sperm as they pass through the woman's reproductive tract.

4. A healthy fallopian tube that will promote the passage of sperm and eggs.

5. A healthy uterine cavity with no abnormalities that might hinder implantation of the embryo.

Couples who cannot fulfill all five criteria probably are unable to conceive naturally. The following section examines some of the ways in which common organic and physiologic problems may prevent a couple from meeting one or more of these criteria. The remainder of this chapter explains how IVF can compensate for many of these deficiencies and thus enable a heretofore infertile couple to conceive; it concludes with a description of the factors that most strongly determine a couple's chance of success with IVF.

Organic and Physiologic Problems That May Prevent Couples from Conceiving Naturally

Neither sex contributes more heavily than the other to these problems. Roughly one-third of all infertile couples can trace their infertility to the woman, one-third to the man, and one-third to both partners.

Some Causes of Female Infertility

The most common cause of infertility in a woman is damaged or blocked fallopian tubes that prevent the egg and sperm from uniting. As mentioned in Chapter 1, sexually transmitted diseases frequently cause tubal scarring and blockage. Conditions such as *endometriosis,* in which the lining of the uterus grows outside the womb (causing scarring, pain, and heavy bleeding), can also damage the fallopian tubes and ovaries. In addition, scar tissue that forms after pelvic surgery may also lead to fertility problems.

Damaged ovaries may also contribute to infertility. Sometimes an ovary cannot release an egg even though hormonal production is normal and the egg is adequately developed. It is possible for an egg to be trapped within the follicle by scarring or thickening of the ovary's surface; this relatively rare condition may either be hereditary or could be induced by the malfunctioning of structures such as the adrenal gland.

More commonly, diseases such as pelvic inflammatory disease or endometriosis, as well as surgically induced scarring, may anchor the ovaries in an awkward position or form a barrier that prevents the fimbriae from applying themselves properly to the ovary's surface. Although one or both of the fallopian tubes may be perfectly free and mobile, the corresponding ovary could be inaccessible and unmovable. In such cases, the egg or eggs would be ovulated into the abdominal cavity instead of being retrieved by the fimbriae.

Abnormal ovulation is another common cause of female infertility. Some women do not ovulate at all, while others ovulate too early or too late in their cycle for a pregnancy to occur and survive. The reason that normal fertility usually wanes after age 35 is largely because ovulation tends to become abnormal later in the childbearing years. In addition it is believed that the quality of eggs decreases as women get older because the eggs' meiotic capacities are diminished by the aging process.

A woman may also be infertile because disease, surgery, or infection have damaged the lining of her uterus. Damage caused by scarring or the presence of tumors, such as fibroids, prevent the embryo from attaching to the endometrium and developing properly.

Abnormalities in the size and shape of the uterus can also cause infertility problems. Sometimes women develop an abnormally shaped uterus as a result of exposure to certain drugs their mothers took during pregnancy. A classic example of this disorder is the "T-shaped" uterus and significantly smaller uterine cavity often found in women whose mothers took diethylstilbestrol (DES) during pregnancy.

Some women are unable to produce the cervical mucus that ensures the passage and vitality of the sperm. The production of hostile cervical mucus might be due to infection or abnormal physical and chemical properties in the secretions. Occasionally, surgery or injury to the cervix may have destroyed the glands that produce cervical secretions.

In some cases, women develop antibodies or an allergic response to their partner's sperm. These antibodies may be passed into the cervical secretions and thereby prevent fertilization by destroying or immobilizing the sperm.

Some Causes of Male Infertility

The causes of male infertility are often more difficult to define. Blockage of the sperm ducts is one obvious cause. Generalized blockage may be caused by sexually transmitted diseases. More easily identifiable blockage is caused by a *vasectomy* (voluntary surgery to occlude the sperm ducts for birth-control purposes). While it is usually possible to surgically reconnect the tubes after vasectomy, some men, especially those who underwent the procedure more than five years earlier, remain infertile because in the interim their systems have developed antibodies that destroy or immobilize their own sperm.

Another common cause of male infertility is a *varicocele,* a collection of dilated veins around the testicles that hinders sperm function by increasing body temperature in the scrotum. In order for the testicles to produce healthy sperm, the temperature in the scrotum must be lower than it is in the rest of the body.

Ideally the testicles should have descended into the scrotum shortly after birth, but in some cases they do not reach the scrotum for years. In such circumstances it may be necessary to accomplish this surgically within early life lest the testicles become irrevocably damaged, resulting in permanent infertility. In rare cases abnormal development of the testicles and/or sperm ducts may result from injury, disease, or hereditary abnormalities.

Certain drugs or chemicals in the environment may also inhibit sperm production and function. And as in women, drugs such as DES can also produce abnormalities in the male offspring's reproductive system.

Finally, for reasons that are often not readily apparent, some men lack the adequate hormonal stimulation that is required for proper sperm production.

Unexplained Infertility

For about 10 percent of all infertile couples, the cause of the infertility cannot be readily determined by conventional diagnostic procedures. Such cases are referred to as "unexplained infertility." Modern IVF technology is making great strides in helping identify some of the causes of so-called unexplained infertility.

How IVF Differs from Natural Conception

This section provides an overview of how IVF adapts the principles of human reproduction to achieve pregnancy. The procedures are described here in general terms and will be discussed in detail in subsequent chapters.

Fertility Drugs Are Used to Produce More Eggs

The administration of fertility drugs promotes the growth of more follicles than would develop naturally. These drugs also enable more follicles and eggs to mature instead of regressing prior to ovulation. Increasing the number of mature follicles facilitates the retrieval of more eggs and enhances the chance of fertilizing more healthy embryos.

Although an embryo has approximately a 30 percent chance of surviving longer than two weeks in nature, an embryo transferred into the uterus during IVF has no more than an 8 to 10 percent chance of survival. Because of the IVF embryo's lower odds of surviving, many programs transfer several embryos at one time into the uterus in order to give the couple a better opportunity of conceiving.

The Chance of a Multiple Pregnancy Is Greater with IVF

Not only is the success rate of an IVF procedure directly related to the number of embryos that are transferred to the woman's uterus, but the more embryos transferred = the more potential fetuses. The tradeoff is obvious: the more embryos transferred = the greater the risk of twins, triplets, or even larger multiples. (See Chapter 4 for a discussion of the risks of multiple pregnancies and the options available to couples who are confronted with a large multiple pregnancy.)

Eggs Are Retrieved from the Ovaries by Suction

Instead of waiting for the eggs to be ovulated naturally from the follicles, the IVF surgeon sucks them out of the ovaries through a long needle in a process known as *egg retrieval*. The needle can be inserted into the follicles during a surgical procedure called *laparoscopy,* or it can be passed through the vagina or urethra into the follicles while the physician monitors its progress on a TV-like *ultrasound* screen (see Chapter 6). The eggs are then sent to the laboratory for fertilization. Egg retrieval is particularly appropriate when the fallopian tubes cannot retrieve or transport the eggs, when the woman is not able to ovulate properly, or in cases of unexplained infertility.

IVF Bypasses the Fallopian Tubes

The fallopian tubes are entirely bypassed because the eggs are retrieved directly from the ovaries, and the fertilized embryos are transferred directly into the uterus. This is why IVF is particularly suited to women who have damaged or blocked fallopian tubes.

Sperm are Partially Capacitated in the Laboratory Instead of in the Woman's Reproductive Tract

In vitro fertilization eliminates many of the hurdles that sperm have to overcome, including escaping from the man's semen and passing through the cervical mucus. This is particularly important in cases where the man has an inadequate sperm count or poor sperm function. In vitro fertilization is also helpful in situations when the woman forms cervical mucus that inadequately promotes capacitation or is hostile to the sperm. Because IVF bypasses the cervix both by substituting laboratory procedures for the role of cervical mucus and again when the embryos are transferred directly into the uterus, negative impacts of the cervical mucus are avoided.

An IVF Embryo Is Not Likely to React to Either Partner's Antibodies

The body sometimes develops antibodies to sperm after it has become familiar with the spermatic blueprint. Accordingly, as sperm come into contact with bodily immune systems over time, women may build up sperm antibodies, and men may even develop antibodies to their own sperm.

In vitro fertilization often avoids fertility problems caused by antibodies produced by the man and/or woman. It enables sperm to safely fertilize the eggs in the laboratory without interference from antibodies that would be present in the woman's reproductive tract. The resulting embryos are not affected by those antibodies because mammalian embryos do not have an immunological blueprint; embryos and fetuses are immunologically inert prior to birth. Thus, the woman's body, which might produce antibodies against sperm, tolerates the embryo because it is an unfamiliar, immunologically inert structure against which her body has not yet developed antibodies.

Abnormalities Are No More Likely to Occur with IVF

Nature seems to have decreed that an embryo conceived in vitro must be exceptionally healthy and unblemished in order to survive. For example, keep in mind that an IVF embryo is placed in the uterus a few days earlier in the menstrual cycle than it would normally reach the uterus after being fertilized in the fallopian tube. The embryo is also less developed at the time of transfer than it would be when it reaches the uterus under normal conditions. In addition, introducing an embryo into an artificially induced hormonal environment (a cycle in which a woman has received fertility drugs) may increase the chances of a luteal phase defect. Therefore, an unhealthy IVF embryo is even less likely to implant than is a healthy one.

Recent studies would indicate that the risk of abnormalities with IVF is less than half of the 2.5 percent abnormality rate that occurs in nature. In fact, only a handful of major congenital abnormalities have occurred in the IVF births reported worldwide following IVF. This is so in spite of the fact that women conceiving with IVF are often over 35, when the risk of abnormalities such as Down's syndrome and other chromosomal defects may be as high as 1 in 200 in the population of babies born to women over 35 in the natural setting.

The same need for an IVF embryo to be especially hardy in order to implant and flourish has resulted in the birth of slightly more girls than boys from IVF. This is because, in addition to nature's slight statistical bias toward girl babies, female embryos and fetuses tend to be hardier than males.

IVF Is Both a Treatment and a Diagnostic Procedure

In vitro fertilization has a built-in diagnostic capability that is unmatched in nature or by any other method of treating infertility. In ideal circumstances there is a 70 percent or greater chance that any one egg will fertilize in the laboratory. This affords the couple a chance to see whether they are capable of achieving fertilization together. In vitro fertilization technology has brought to light many instances in which a woman's egg cannot be fertilized by her partner's sperm and sometimes not by any sperm. The reason for this is not always readily identifiable; the problem could lie with the egg, the sperm, or both. A couple in this situation might choose to abandon further treatment; or the next time around they might consider using donor sperm, donor eggs, or donor embryos (see Chapter 11). No other method of treating infertility enables a physician to reach this diagnostic conclusion.

Another diagnostic application of IVF would be when, for no readily apparent reason, the fallopian tubes might be unable to properly receive and/or transport the eggs, sperm, and embryos. Because IVF by its very nature bypasses the fallopian tubes, it might—through a process of exclusion—offer both an answer and/or a solution to this problem.

IVF Exacts a Heavy Emotional, Physical, and Financial Investment

The most significant difference between IVF and natural pregnancy is that a couple must sacrifice a great deal of their personal privacy before and during the IVF procedure, whereas natural conception is a private matter. An IVF couple must bare some of their deepest secrets and fears to the clinic staff, and allow themselves to be manipulated physically and emotionally as they progress through the procedure. In addition, IVF is inordinately expensive—and there is no second prize if a woman does not conceive following in vitro. The couple will not have another chance at pregnancy without making the same emotional, physical, and financial investment again. In natural conception, there's always next month, and the next month, and hope for the future without the major cost that in vitro exacts.

Who Are Most Likely to Be Successful IVF Candidates?

The success rate with IVF depends upon many factors, most of which have not been clearly defined. However, the following factors strongly influence the infertile couple's chance of successful IVF.

The Woman Is Not Nearing the Menopause

The closer the woman is to the menopause the more difficult it is to achieve optimal stimulation with fertility drugs. Hence, it is the woman's proximity to the menopause rather than her absolute age that impacts on the IVF pregnancy rate. For example, a woman who is going to experience an early menopause around age 40 would react like an older woman in terms of her potential success with IVF while still in her thirties; conversely, a woman who may not go through menopause until age 55 might at age 40 respond to fertility drugs like a 30-year-old. Since most women experience the menopause around age 50, women who are over 40 tend to have a significantly reduced IVF pregnancy rate; we have observed that women under 40 are almost twice as likely to become pregnant with IVF as are those over 40.

Accordingly, chronological age impacts IVF success rates only insofar as it affects the woman's ability to (1) be stimulated with fertility drugs, (2) develop a number of healthy follicles with good eggs, and (3) produce eggs that are fertilizable. This may be attributable to the fact that as women get older their ability to produce healthy eggs declines. In addition, the woman's lifetime quota of eggs may be impacted by the normal aging process. However, with the advent of new drugs it may become possible to enhance even the older woman's response to fertility drugs.

The Infertility Is Caused by Female Pelvic Disease

The chances of pregnancy with IVF are highest in cases where the infertility is exclusively due to blocked or irreparably damaged fallopian tubes, and all other parameters are normal.

The Woman Has a Large, Healthy Uterus

The size, health, and shape of the uterus are critical. Women with fibroid tumors of the uterus, polyps (outgrowths that protrude into the uterine cavity), fibrous bands that alter its shape, or other disorders that have destroyed the integrity of the uterine wall tend to have lower pregnancy rates. Women who were exposed to drugs such as DES during their own gestation also are less successful with IVF. Finally, women with normally shaped but exceptionally small uteruses have, in our experience, a much lower pregnancy rate.

The Woman Has Both Ovaries

The ability of the ovaries to produce follicles in response to stimulation by fertility drugs is a priority because the number of follicles produced = the number of eggs that can be retrieved = number of embryos available to transfer. The woman's chances for success would be diminished if one ovary or even part of one has been removed surgically, or if she was born with only one ovary. Other complicating factors include ovarian failure (ovaries that do not function properly), diseases elsewhere in the body that may affect the ovaries, the woman's general hormonal balance, and the quality of her eggs.

The Woman Has Had One or More Pregnancies

If the woman has been pregnant before it can be assumed that her eggs probably will fertilize again. If she has not been pregnant before, inherent genetic or structural egg defects that might not be microscopically detectable can only be identified when fertilization fails to occur in the laboratory.

If she was previously pregnant by her current partner it is probable that his sperm will fertilize her eggs, but if she has not been impregnated by him it is not possible to determine prior to IVF how her eggs will respond to his sperm.

In addition, a woman is likely to have an adequately large uterus if it has already been stretched by an earlier pregnancy. Also, women who have had babies are less likely to have fibroid tumors of the uterus because pregnancy usually protects against their development.

The Man Has Healthy Sperm

Finally, if the male partner has strong, fertile sperm (a normal sperm count with good motility) and no other male fertility problems, the likelihood of success will increase. In our experience, when the man has a concentration of healthy motile sperm less than 10 million per ml, its fertilization ability begins to decline because the sperm's potential for fertilizing seems to be linked to the concentration of motile sperm. The normal concentration of motile sperm in any healthy male is about 50 percent or greater; in other words, if a man has a sperm count of 100 million he could expect to have 50 million motile sperm. New laboratory techniques for improving the motility of sperm offer hope for men with a reduced concentration of motile sperm. In addition, new processing techniques in the laboratory facilitate the removal of some sperm antibodies that also may impact fertilization.

Summary

The ideal IVF candidates would be a couple who meet all of these criteria: a woman not nearing menopause who is healthy, ovulates regularly, and has normal hormonal function; whose infertility is due to blocked or irreparably damaged fallopian tubes; who has a healthy uterus of normal size and shape, and two normal ovaries; and who has proved that her eggs can be fertilized by having conceived some time in the past—and a man who is perfectly fertile.

The most likely candidates for IVF are couples whose infertility is caused by tubal damage and/or blockage, all other factors being equal. Couples whose infertility is related to male subfertility problems, even if the woman's tubes are normal, have a lower chance of getting pregnant following IVF than do couples where the cause of infertility relates to female organic disease. Finally, the lowest success rate is reported for couples with unexplained infertility because, among other causes, unexplained infertility may be due to an inability of the egg to be fertilized.

This does not necessarily mean that couples who do not meet all six criteria, or even four or five, should despair. Depending on the couple's particular set of circumstances, the physician can compensate for the lack of or deficiency in some of the criteria by employing today's high-tech procedures. For example, although both the number and quality of eggs tend to decrease with age, a woman over 40 with a large, healthy uterus and the proper hormonal environment may become pregnant even if the laboratory is able to fertilize only one or two eggs. Chapter 9, "Shaping Reasonable Expectations about IVF," discusses some of the ways that IVF can be used to help couples become pregnant although they do not fulfill all of these criteria to the letter.

PART II

How IVF Is Performed

CHAPTER 4

IVF Step 1: Preparation for Treatment

Most IVF procedures are based on some variation of the following steps: (1) preparation for treatment, (2) induction of ovulation, (3) egg retrieval, and (4) embryo transfer. All successful IVF programs must be highly organized and exquisitely timed, just as the fertilization process is organized and timed in nature.

Each of these four basic steps in an IVF treatment cycle should be regarded as a hurdle that a couple must overcome before proceeding further. (The term *treatment cycle* refers to the menstrual cycle during which a particular IVF procedure is performed.) Occasionally, a couple may successfully negotiate one hurdle but then be unable to overcome the next step; in such a case they would usually begin the treatment cycle anew after a month or two. In general, a couple's chances for successful IVF increase as they put each hurdle behind them.

The descriptions of IVF procedures in Chapters 4 to 7 have been designed to provide an overview of what an infertile couple might expect to experience physically and emotionally during a treatment cycle. Because a truly comprehensive IVF program responds to—and often anticipates—the couple's emotional needs throughout the treatment cycle, some of the techniques that an IVF program might use to address emotional needs are included in the description of clinical procedures. We do not mean to imply that any of these scenarios is the best or only way that IVF should be performed.

Acceptance into an IVF Program

Before being admitted into a hypothetical IVF program, the couple would probably be required to have a complete medical workup. They would most likely undergo all the routine steps of an infertility assessment, usually performed by their own primary physician, in order to rule out the possibility that procedures other than IVF might better address their needs. (Chapters 8 and 11 discuss the advisability of exhausting all other options before selecting IVF.)

The couple would probably be required to forward their medical records to the IVF program and are likely to be asked to provide additional background by telephone. They should expect to be encouraged to speak frankly about themselves and their personal habits (including their sexual practices, use and abuse of recreational drugs, general life-style, and other parameters that are known to impact fertility). In many programs, including ours, the couple also would be asked to complete detailed psychological inventories. Following a thorough evaluation of the materials submitted by the couple and their primary physician, the medical staff would then decide whether the couple are eligible for IVF.

Once accepted into the program, the couple would probably undergo some orientation, including an explanation of the emotional, physical, and financial commitments that IVF would require. This orientation could take place through letters, other written material, or by telephone; or it may occur on-site if the couple are able to visit the clinic prior to commencement of the treatment cycle.

In some programs the couple have to be at the clinic during the entire process, including *induction of ovulation* (usually a series of daily injections). In other programs the couples are encouraged to initiate the induction of ovulation with their own gynecologist, and are required to be on-site only for the last few days of the cycle prior to egg retrieval and embryo transfer.

Organization of a Typical IVF Program

In many programs one or more nurse-coordinators play an important role in assisting the physician to ensure that the couple receive proper emotional preparation throughout the program. The nurse-coordinators, who are highly trained professionals, play a central role and administer many treatment procedures that previously were agreed upon by the entire medical staff.

In such a coordinator-oriented program, the couple could anticipate spending as much if not more time with a nurse-coordinator than they would with the physician. This is because a nurse-coordinator usually functions as the couple's advocate—the liaison between the couple and all the other members of the IVF team including the physician. However, this is not meant to imply that both the clinical and administrative roles could not be fulfilled by a physician who has a personality and attitude that will engender a feeling of well-being, relaxation, and optimism. In general, though, nurse-coordinators contribute significantly to the smooth operation of many IVF programs.

It is the responsibility of the person who guides the couple throughout the treatment cycle, whether physician or nurse-coordinator, to explain every step along the way so the couple know exactly what to expect. In addition, the same staff member who is responsible for establishing the initial rapport with the couple should be their contact person throughout their tenure with the program.

In most programs the couple will be introduced to the staff, taken on a tour of the facility, and encouraged to ask a lot of questions. The staff in an IVF program, including the clerical personnel, should be upbeat and encouraging when they deal with infertile couples. The empathic IVF program will provide a relaxing, low-key environment that offers subtle support to both partners during their time of emotional need. Although the couple should be well aware that no program can guarantee a pregnancy, even after several attempts, a congenial atmosphere fostered by the staff should help both partners maintain a mood of guarded optimism.

Some programs, including ours, have access to a counselor with special expertise in the psychological aspects of infertility. Although the participation of a counselor is not essential in order for a couple to conceive, an IVF team member who can predict the way a couple might react, and therefore help improve their tolerance to the emotional roller-coaster ride of IVF, adds another dimension of caring to the program.

Tests That May Be Conducted Prior to IVF

Before the couple have a pretreatment consultation with the physician, it is likely that they will be asked to complete some or all of the following tests.

The AIDS Test

In today's climate, a couple should defer pregnancy until they are sure that neither partner carries a disease that can seriously prejudice the health, well-being, and even the survival of the offspring. Although this is a personal decision to be resolved between the man and woman, the physician enters the picture when IVF is being considered. As the catalyst responsible for creating the circumstances under which a new life might be conceived, the physician has a medical, legal, and moral obligation to make every attempt to ensure that IVF does not lead to the birth of a child who suffers from a life-endangering disease such as AIDS.

Accordingly, many programs, including ours, require that an AIDS test be done on both partners prior to any IVF procedure. Unfortunately, this test still does not completely rule out the presence of AIDS because a person may not register positive for up to six months after infection by the AIDS virus. However, the test does provide a good screen to help protect an IVF program from being instrumental in the birth of damaged offspring.

Another reason for administering the AIDS test to all new patients is to protect medical and laboratory personnel who work with the couple. Richard Marrs, M.D., the director of a respected IVF program in Los Angeles and one of the leading experts in the field of IVF, expressed his concern about AIDS at a 1987 IVF conference in Reno, Nevada:

> AIDS screening is extremely important now not only for the protection of the personnel that are handling the follicular fluid, the serum, the blood, the semen samples, but also in patients who are coming through treatment, whether it is by GIFT (gamete intrafallopian transfer) or other reproductive technologies such as intrauterine insemination.... If you don't have an ongoing screening program on a regular basis, and patients turn positive under your care, you may have more difficulty protecting yourself as well as the workers within your program.

Some physicians also test both partners for AIDS before the woman undergoes any treatment to enhance fertility, such as reconstructive tubal surgery. This is because if one of the partners is AIDS-positive and a baby with AIDS is born after successful tubal surgery, the couple might argue that they would not have consented to treatment had they known they could transmit AIDS to a baby. We recognize that the decision to undergo AIDS testing is a very personal one and that a physician certainly cannot force anyone to have this test; nevertheless, we strongly advise that the issue be discussed prior to initiating treatment for infertility.

Some IVF couples have expressed concern that AIDS might be transmitted through fertility drugs because these drugs are derived from the urine of menopausal women. Most experts agree, however, that the AIDS virus does not survive the purification and extraction process to which these drugs are subjected.

The Sperm Count

In any IVF program the male partner will almost certainly be asked to submit to a sperm count. The purpose of the sperm count is twofold: (1) to ensure that the sperm's viability and motility are not abnormal and/or have not changed significantly since the last sperm count, which would dramatically affect the couple's rational expectations for successful IVF, and (2) to protect the program from medical-legal liability in case the man has developed an undetected fertility problem since his sperm were last evaluated.

The Sperm Antibody Test

More and more programs, including ours, increasingly require that both partners undergo sperm antibody tests to determine whether they harbor these antibodies. This test is important because if the woman's blood is to be used in the laboratory medium in which the eggs are fertilized and the embryos are cultured, the presence of antibodies to her partner's sperm must first be ruled out. If her blood does contain antibodies that would preclude fertilization, donor blood may have to be substituted. Although careful screening should rule out any possibility that contaminated donor blood would be substituted in such a case, the couple nevertheless should be made aware of the implications for the offspring should contaminated blood be used accidentally.

Some IVF programs prepare the growth medium from blood obtained from the umbilical cords of newborn babies in nearby hospitals. However, the use of cord blood, unless very carefully screened and controlled, again opens the door to possible AIDS and hepatitis virus contamination. For this reason, as well as from an emotional/psychological point of view, we prefer to use the woman's own blood whenever possible.

The Pretreatment Consultation

Once the appropriate tests have been completed the physician and perhaps the nurse-coordinator will discuss with the couple what to expect throughout the treatment cycle. Although the couple may have a general idea, the physician will reinforce what they have already been told and will encourage them to ask questions.

The physician probably will also outline some of the decisions the couple will have to make in the next few days. These include: (1) how many eggs they wish to have fertilized; (2) what they want to do with any excess eggs; (3) how many embryos they want to have transferred into the uterus; (4) how they wish to dispose of any excess embryos; and (5) how they would deal with a large multiple pregnancy (quadruplets or larger), should that occur. Although these questions do not all have to be answered at the same time, the physician probably will touch on all of the relevant issues during this consultation in order to give the couple ample time to prepare themselves to make their decisions.

Preparing for the Inevitable Tradeoff: Probability of Pregnancy versus the Risk of Multiple Births

Because an embryo's chances of survival, even in the best circumstances, are only about 8 to 10 percent, it is obvious that enough embryos must be transferred into the uterus to ensure the highest probable birthrate. Some programs transfer a maximum of three or four at a time, others as many as six. It has been our experience that placement of four embryos in the uterus yields a 25 to 30 percent probability of success.

However, the couple wishing to maximize their chances of pregnancy must be prepared to confront the unavoidable tradeoff: the more embryos the greater the risk of multiple births. The multiple birthrate from IVF is twins in about one out of every three pregnancies, triplets in one out of every ten—and one out of every forty couples will have quadruplets or more.

The Risks of a Multiple Pregnancy

The couple must be thoroughly educated on the implications of multiple pregnancy before they decide how many embryos to have transferred. While most healthy women can tolerate a triplet pregnancy, a larger multiple pregnancy threatens the well-being of both mother and babies. Moreover, the risks become greater to both mother and babies as the number of fetuses increases.

Risks to the mother that are especially acute during a large multiple pregnancy include high blood pressure, uterine bleeding, and problems associated with a cesarean section (the incidence of cesarean sections increases dramatically in multiple pregnancies).

The primary threat to the physical and intellectual well-being of the babies stems from complications resulting from premature birth. Multiple births often occur prematurely; and the more babies the more premature the birth. Prematurity can cause one and possibly all of the babies to be born brain-damaged and/or with a dangerously low birth weight that can endanger the child's survival. Although the widespread belief that even IVF babies born from a nonmultiple pregnancy have small birth weights is a myth, it is true that one or more of the babies in an IVF multiple are often small—however, this is the case in natural multiple pregnancies as well.

Selective Reduction of Pregnancy
Because of the serious complications that so often occur in large multiple pregnancies, some IVF programs counsel couples on the concept of selectively reducing the size of a multiple pregnancy as a possible lifesaving measure to the remaining fetuses.

Selective reduction of pregnancy, which is usually performed prior to completion of the third month of gestation, involves the injection of a chemical under guidance by ultrasound directly into one or more developing fetuses. This causes the involved fetus or fetuses to succumb almost immediately, and they are subsequently absorbed by the body. Selective reduction of pregnancy is unlikely to cause a miscarriage in the remaining fetuses—provided that it is done by an expert.

IVF programs might be considered pro-life because IVF by its very nature is the opposite of abortion. Yet, many physicians who perform IVF believe strongly that abortion in the interest of saving life is acceptable, or at least presents a possible option. We believe that couples should be made aware, in an unbiased manner, about the option of selective termination of pregnancy in a pro-choice environment.

Constructing a Framework for Decision-Making
Before the couple can decide how many eggs should be fertilized after egg retrieval, they first have to decide whether they are willing to risk a multiple pregnancy. At this point, the physician might say to them:

There is a difference of opinion as to how many embryos should be transferred into the uterus. What you need to remember is that there is a tradeoff. If you put in more embryos you have a higher chance of pregnancy up to a maximum of four. We have found that the pregnancy rate does not increase beyond four.

How many embryos are you going to want? Because we can usually fertilize between 70 to 80 percent of the eggs that we retrieve, we would encourage you to have at least six or seven eggs fertilized if you want four embryos transferred. If you want four embryos but fertilize only four eggs, you may only end up with no more than two or three embryos; that's the chance you take.

If you want to be sure of having only one baby, we have to transfer just one embryo. That's the only way we can promise you just one baby—but you then only have an 8 percent chance of getting pregnant. If you want two babies maximum, we cannot put in more than two embryos. You must be prepared to deal with the consequences of a multiple pregnancy or else transfer no more embryos than you are willing to have develop into babies.

The couple who want four embryos to be transferred thus have two choices: (1) to fertilize only four eggs to preclude the development of more than four embryos (but possibly ending up with only two or three) or (2) to fertilize more than four eggs in order to have four healthy embryos.

If the couple are willing to risk a multiple pregnancy, the physician may then ask whether they would consider selective pregnancy reduction should it become necessary. If they agree to the concept of selective pregnancy reduction, the physician might be satisfied to subsequently transfer four embryos. Some couples, for moral, ethical, or religious reasons (or simply because they want to enhance their chance of conceiving), want every embryo transferred but refuse to consider selective pregnancy reduction; that is their choice. In such cases, the physician is likely to agree to transfer as many embryos as the couple request but could be expected to ask them to sign a release.

This is a particularly crucial discussion because it leads to related decisions. For example, what if all the eggs fertilize, resulting in eight or nine embryos? If four are transferred, what should be done with the remainder? Should they be frozen for IVF use during a subsequent menstrual cycle? Should they be donated to another couple? Might they be used for research? Or should they be discarded? The same questions apply to eggs that the couple choose not to have fertilized.

Decision: How Many Eggs Should be Fertilized?
Although some of these difficult decisions can be postponed until immediately prior to embryo transfer, the couple must decide during this consultation or shortly thereafter how many eggs to fertilize and what should be done with any excess eggs. This is because physicians are not allowed to get consent from a woman after she has been premedicated for surgery (the egg retrieval, in this case), and her partner should not make such a decision alone. The decision cannot be made after egg retrieval because the laboratory must begin to process eggs and sperm often before the woman will have fully recovered from the anesthesia. Therefore, it is necessary for both partners to decide together, prior to egg retrieval (preferably the day before); and their decision should be documented.

The couple can delay deciding about how many embryos to transfer, how they wish to dispose of any excess embryos, and how they intend to deal with a large multiple pregnancy— but only until immediately before the embryo transfer. However, they would be well advised to thoroughly discuss their feelings and preferences in the interim because all of these decisions are fundamentally interrelated.

CHAPTER 5

IVF Step 2: Induction of Ovulation

A woman undergoing IVF is given fertility drugs for two reasons: (1) to enhance the growth and development of her ovarian follicles in order to produce as many healthy eggs as possible and (2) to control the timing of ovulation so the eggs can be surgically retrieved before they are ovulated. In vitro fertilization is rarely performed in natural cycles (cycles in which no fertility drugs are administered) because in such cases it is unlikely that more than one or two eggs can be retrieved at a time.

The ovulation of more than one egg, which has been induced through the administration of fertility drugs, is known as *superovulation*. The term *controlled ovarian hyperstimulation* (COH) encompasses the concept of superovulation but also refers to production of an exaggerated hormonal response that favors implantation of the embryo into the endometrium. The terms stimulation, superovulation, and controlled ovarian hyperstimulation are often used interchangeably; when a specific term is used in this book, it is intended to convey a slightly different emphasis.

The degree to which the woman is stimulated is measured by the concentration of the hormone estrogen (the *estradiol*, or E_2 level) in her blood and/or visualization of the developing ovarian follicles by ultrasound. It has been shown that the greater the degree of controlled ovarian hyperstimulation, the more eggs will be available for retrieval.

Ovulation can be expected to occur about 38 hours after a woman is optimally stimulated. Egg retrieval therefore has to be scheduled for a few hours prior to the anticipated time of ovulation so the eggs can be retrieved *before* being expelled into the abdominal cavity. As will be explained later in this chapter, the methods of assessing the degree of stimulation, predicting the time of ovulation, or inducing ovulation vary according to the fertility drug used.

Induction of ovulation makes physical and emotional demands on the couple. The woman should expect to undergo daily administration of a fertility drug, usually by injection, as well as blood tests and/or ultrasound evaluations to monitor her progress. In addition, both partners should be prepared to cope with the strong emotions that some women experience because of the hormonal changes introduced by the fertility drugs. As one nurse-coordinator explained:

> It doesn't take anything to make women emotional at this point. I have at least one patient a week sobbing in my office just looking at the plants. Sometimes they will even cry over dog-food commercials. The couple have to be prepared for this, and the man should be especially supportive and tolerant.

Two Approaches to Induction of Ovulation

There are two equally acceptable philosophies with regard to the induction of ovulation: a "chef-like" and a "recipe-like" approach. In the chef-like approach the hormonal dosage administered is tailored to each woman's unique circumstances, much as a chef might modify a recipe to fit the situation. In the recipe-like approach patients are assigned to one of several protocols based upon clinical and hormonal evaluations. The protocol rigidly defines the type, dosage, and method of stimulation with fertility agents as well as the entire sequence, timing, and process of treatment. We find the recipe-like approach is better suited to our program because we feel that following a rigid protocol guarantees quality control. In addition, we believe that the recipe-like approach facilitates the transfer of knowledge and information to others who will be able to replicate our success.

Fertility Drug Therapies

The following section outlines the most common fertility drugs used in the United States. In general, the woman's response to these drugs will depend on her pattern of ovulation and her age.

Clomiphene Citrate

Until recently the use of clomiphene citrate was the most popular method of inducing ovulation. *Clomiphene citrate* is a synthetic hormone that deceives the hypothalamus into thinking that the body's estrogen level is too low. In response, the hypothalamus releases GnRH (gonadotropin-releasing hormone), which in turn prompts the pituitary gland to release an exaggerated amount of FSH. As happens in nature, the increased secretion of FSH stimulates development of the follicles, ultimately resulting in ovulation. The growing follicles secrete estrogen into the bloodstream, thus closing the feedback circle that the hypothalamus initiated in response to the antiestrogen properties of clomiphene.

Administration of clomiphene citrate enhances the normal cyclical pattern of follicular development and ovulation. If initiated as early as day 2 of the menstrual cycle, it usually induces ovulation on day 13 or 14 of a regular 28-day cycle; if administered later, such as on day 5, ovulation could occur as late as day 16 or 17, and the length of the cycle may be extended. If the woman does not stimulate appropriately on the original dosage of clomiphene, the dosage may be increased to achieve optimal stimulation. We often administer hCG to the patient once ultrasound examinations and hormonal evaluations confirm optimal follicular development. In such cases ovulation will usually occur about 38 hours later.

Two major advantages of clomiphene are its relatively low cost and the fact that it can be taken orally instead of by injection. A distinct disadvantage is that when administered alone it does not stimulate the growth and maturation of as many follicles as do alternative therapies such as *human menopausal gonadotropin* (hMG) or clomiphene plus hMG; accordingly, fewer eggs can be retrieved.

Side Effects of Clomiphene
The side effects associated with clomiphene are related to the follicular development the drug has stimulated. When administered alone, a luteal-phase defect may result if the follicles do not develop properly; this would hinder implantation by preventing the endometrium from responding optimally to progesterone produced by the corpus luteum. Clomiphene may also interfere with the nurturing effect that estrogen must have on the developing endometrium.

In addition, traces of clomiphene that might linger in the woman's circulatory system for many weeks may inhibit the normal function of enzymes produced by the developing follicular cells.

Too high a dose of clomiphene may cause follicles to grow too rapidly, producing large fluid-filled collections or cysts. This may lead to tenderness and swelling of the ovaries, visual disturbances, and hot flashes similar to those at menopause may be experienced.

Finally, a too high dose of clomiphene may decrease the amount of cervical mucus produced and may also reduce its quality, with negative implications for the passage and capacitation of the sperm.

Safety of Clomiphene
Some recent studies have suggested that clomiphene citrate has caused birth defects or a higher miscarriage rate in labo-

ratory animals and could, therefore, potentially threaten human offspring. We, however, believe that when clomiphene is taken under proper supervision these risks should not be of major significance.

The fear that clomiphene might cause birth defects arises from the fact that its inner structure, or nucleus, is very similar to that of the hormone DES, which is known to have caused so many birth defects when administered to pregnant women.

Although it is theoretically possible that clomiphene might cause such defects, birth statistics do not indicate an increased birth-defect rate after stimulation with this fertility drug. The laboratory studies mentioned above should not be ignored, however, but should be heeded as a guide to safe, prudent administration of fertility drugs.

We caution that clomiphene citrate should only be taken when it is absolutely certain that the woman is not pregnant. (The appearance of a menstrual period does not provide adequate certainty because more than 10 percent of women might bleed during early pregnancy; assessment by a physician or even a home pregnancy test provide greater assurance that a pregnancy does not exist.)

One of the anti-estrogenic components of clomiphene tends to accumulate in the woman's body over time. Accordingly, the administration of clomiphene as a fertility agent over a series of months might potentiate infertility. Furthermore, repeated administration without proper scrutiny may create potential risks. Therefore, the practice of physicians saying to patients, "Here's some clomiphene. Take some each month and call me if you miss your period" should be denounced.

But if clomiphene citrate is taken under proper supervision and the woman has determined that she is not pregnant, its safety is beyond question. This has prompted many IVF programs to continue using clomiphene; however, they invariably report a lower pregnancy rate than that which can be achieved by other methods of controlled ovarian hyperstimulation.

Human Menopausal Gonadotropin (hMG)

This fertility drug contains equal amounts of the gonadotropins FSH and LH. It is derived from the urine of menopausal women, a good source of both FSH and LH. It is likely that vastly improved hMG produced by microorganisms subjected to genetic engineering will soon become commercially available. This is because a menopausal woman's pituitary gland, in response to a feedback message that her ovaries are no longer producing enough estrogen, increases the output of FSH and LH in an effort to restimulate the failing ovaries; and the excess FSH and LH are excreted in the urine. Urine used for hMG is distilled, filtered, and purified by an expensive process. At the time this book is being written, one ampule of hMG costs about $35 in the United States, and the average woman might require 15 to 25 ampules per treatment cycle.

Human menopausal gonadotropin, which is used in several successful IVF programs in the United States, is considered to have many advantages. Instead of influencing the hypothalamus and pituitary gland to produce more hormones to stimulate follicular development (as is the case with clomiphene), hMG acts directly on the ovaries. In addition, it does not inhibit the function of estrogen or the enzymes of the cells lining the follicles.

If administered in sufficient amounts beginning early enough in the menstrual cycle, hMG will prompt the maturation of a large number of follicles. Although the average number of eggs usually retrieved after hMG stimulation from a woman with two ovaries is between three and six, retrievals of more than twenty eggs have been reported. The usual injection schedule is from day 2 or 3 to day 8 to 12 of the menstrual cycle. Because hMG cannot be absorbed through the stomach into the bloodstream, it must be administered by injection rather than in pill form.

One of the most significant attributes of hMG is its safety-valve effect on ovulation. No matter how well stimulated a woman becomes when she takes hMG, she will be unlikely to ovulate until she receives an injection of hCG. Thus, if for any reason it is determined that the woman should not progress to ovulation, the hCG is simply not administered.

Side Effects of hMG

Many women report breast tenderness, backaches, headaches, insomnia, bloating, and increased vaginal discharge that is directly due to increased mucus production by the cervix.

Luteal-phase defects (inadequate production of progesterone by the corpus luteum to sustain the endometrium) are also known to occur in association with hMG therapy. However, endometrial biopsies have shown that the development of the uterine lining of patients stimulated with hMG is usually a few days ahead of that which could be expected in unstimulated cycles. Thus, hMG helps to synchronize development of the endometrium with growth of the follicles and eggs. This synchronization is a critical prerequisite for successful implantation because IVF embryos are usually transferred to the uterus a few days earlier than they would reach it under natural circumstances; therefore, accelerated endometrial development enhances the chances that the young embryos will implant after their transfer to the uterus.

Possible side effects of hMG overstimulation that threaten the woman's well-being include enlargement and "weeping" of the ovaries, a condition in which a large amount of fluid is exuded into the abdominal cavity. In severe cases this can cause the abdomen to distend severely and may even compromise breathing. In rare cases the kidneys or liver may fail, and the woman may stop producing urine, which can be life-threatening. In very severe cases her blood may lose its ability to clot properly. These situations, however, are extremely rare and usually are caused by inappropriate use of hMG; they are highly unlikely to occur in the properly managed cycle.

It is significant that hMG is unlikely to produce any serious persistent side effects until the woman receives the injection of hCG to stimulate ovulation. Thus, the physician has ample time to assess her status and withhold the hCG if it appears that she might develop major side effects (an assessment made on the basis of blood estradiol values immediately prior to hCG administration). This built-in protective advantage shields almost all women being treated with hMG (administered either alone or in combination with clomiphene) from the serious hazards of overstimulation (see "The Injection of hCG— A Safety Valve" later in this chapter).

Finally, the entire contents of the follicles are removed during egg retrieval, thus reducing any likelihood that the ovary will "weep." For this reason, serious side effects from hMG are much less likely to occur in IVF patients than in those women who do not subsequently undergo egg retrieval.

Variations in Response to hMG
Some women stimulate well after relatively small doses of hMG; others require two, three, or even four times that dosage to achieve the same effect. At the present time, selecting the proper dosage is a trial-and-error procedure; there is no way to accurately predict how a particular woman will respond. Each woman is unique, and each one will react differently to hMG. However, about 80 percent of all women respond appropriately to an average injection.

Researchers have recently begun to identify and measure certain hormones in the woman's blood that will predict the probable way she will respond to a variety of stimulation methods. These tests may also prove to be of value in selecting the most appropriate fertility drug or combination of fertility drugs to be administered as well as the most appropriate dosage.

At present, however, IVF is still a case of hit-or-miss; so when a woman fails to become stimulated on the first try, hormone tests are indicated to ensure that she is not in the climacteric (on the verge of menopause) as well as to determine if hormonal abnormalities or other conditions might be inhibiting her sensitivity to hMG. If she is not in the climacteric and no other abnormalities are detected, then it can be anticipated that she will eventually respond to an adjusted dosage of hMG. She can begin another round of hMG therapy with an adjusted dosage after she lets her body recover for a month or two. Women who have undergone as many as four attempts with hMG prior to stimulating adequately have subsequently conceived.

The number of eggs that can be retrieved as well as the risk of side effects are directly proportional to the blood-estrogen level rather than the hMG dosage given. Follicle growth and development, egg maturation, and the risk of side effects are directly related to the patient's response as evaluated by blood-estrogen levels and/or ultrasound, not to the dosage. Therefore, it is illogical to fear administering an escalating dose of hMG after a poor response to a standard dosage; what is important is to monitor the *individual's* response to the drug.

The tremendous interpersonal and intrapersonal variations in response to hMG might be attributable to one or both of the following factors. First, it could be that hormonal and biochemical factors governing the response to hMG vary in different women or even at different stages of the same woman's life. For example, age influences the woman's ovarian receptivity to hMG, especially as she nears the climacteric. In addition, some women simply will not respond consistently to administration of the same dosage of hMG from month to month.

A second possible cause of response variation is that separate batches of hMG might have differing bio-potencies. Gonadotropins such as FSH consist of a combination of as many as nine similarly structured components called *iso-hormones;* unfortunately, not all these iso-hormones are biologically equivalent in their activity. Thus, the activity of the iso-hormones may vary from batch to batch of hMG and related drugs. Fortunately, much research is currently under way to identify the active ingredients of gonadotropins and thereby better standardize the bio-potency of these fertility drugs.

Recent research has made it possible to partly correct for interpersonal variation in response to gonadotropins and thus identify the dosage and regimen of stimulation that would best suit each individual. This can be done quite easily a month before a woman's IVF or GIFT treatment cycle by measuring the FSH and LH in her blood. We measure the woman's FSH, LH, and *prolactin* (another hormone, produced by the brain, that influences the activity of FSH on the ovaries) during the menstrual period immediately preceding her treatment cycle. This enables us to better correct for any interpersonal variation in response to hMG, giving our patients approximately an 80 percent chance of stimulating correctly on the first attempt. However, we are unable to correct for the possible variation in sensitivity from one batch of hMG to another.

Another encouraging new approach to this problem of inconsistent reaction has been the introduction of GnRH agonists, which appear to have the ability to regulate the ovaries' response to hMG (see "Promising New Fertility Drugs" later in this chapter).

Combination of Clomiphene and hMG

Many IVF programs today administer a mixture of clomiphene and hMG, and a large number of pregnancies have been reported with this combination. One reason for the widespread use of this combination is that clomiphene increases the ovaries' sensitivity to hMG, thereby reducing the dosage of hMG that must be administered; thus the overall cost of the fertility drugs is significantly decreased by reducing the required amount of expensive hMG. A second reason for administering these drugs in combination is to simplify their administration (clomiphene can be taken in pill form although hMG must be injected).

However, we believe that the administration of this combination has several drawbacks. First, because clomiphene has the ability to induce ovulation, a combination of clomiphene and hMG may cause spontaneous ovulation even without the administration of hCG. In such a case egg retrieval might inadvertently take place after ovulation has occurred, resulting in fewer eggs being retrieved. In addition, some physicians feel that the combination of the two drugs makes it difficult to pinpoint the amounts of each that should be changed when the overall dosage must be adjusted in subsequent treatment cycles.

Side effects associated with the use of hMG and related to the degree of stimulation as measured by estrogen levels also apply to the use of clomiphene plus hMG. Accordingly, proper management of the treatment cycle should limit the risks of side effects from the clomiphene-hMG combination.

Purified FSH

Purified FSH is derived by processing and purifying hMG to eliminate most, if not all, of the LH. Some physicians feel that the LH component might have a negative effect on the woman's response to the hMG, but IVF pregnancy rates (when purified FSH is used) do not support this conclusion. Purified FSH is more expensive than hMG, and there is little evidence that it is more effective than hMG. As with hMG, variations in both interpersonal and intrapersonal responses due to the influence of iso-hormones are known to occur with purified FSH. Purified FSH has advantages in treating selected infertility problems such as ovaries with multiple small cysts (*polycystic ovarian disease*), but this situation rarely applies to the IVF setting.

FSH-hMG-Clomiphene Combinations

Combinations of these three drugs are sometimes used; but until more data are available on pregnancy results from using this therapy, their use is rarely indicated.

Promising New Fertility Drugs

Sometimes women cannot be adequately stimulated by the fertility drugs discussed above. In many cases, this problem is age-related. As explained earlier, ovaries tend to become less responsive to stimulation as women get older and thus closer to the menopause. However, in some women the menopause may occur prematurely (under the age of 40), and these women may show signs of increased resistance to fertility drugs in their thirties. In other cases, women may be resistant to such stimulation because of underlying disorders affecting other hormone-producing glands of the body such as the thyroid and adrenal glands.

Studies show that many of the interpersonal variations in response to fertility drugs occur because some women release higher levels of LH into their blood than others. This finding has led to the suggestion that substances that can inhibit the release of LH in a woman being treated with fertility drugs may help standardize responses to the drugs, both among individuals and from cycle to cycle for the same woman. The drugs that inhibit the release of LH, or *GnRH (gonadotropin-releasing hormone) agonists,* enhance the response to hMG in many women whose ovaries had previously resisted fertility drugs. However, the use of GnRH agonists is still under evaluation.

It is now possible to suppress the output of LH by injecting a GnRH agonist and then combining it with hMG/FSH treatment to stimulate the woman because her body's feedback mechanism will have been defused. No serious long-lasting side effects have been reported although patients have experienced symptoms such as hot flashes, nausea, vomiting, and headaches—all of which disappeared when the therapy was discontinued.

Unfortunately, GnRH agonists are costly, and in addition their administration almost always requires that the relatively expensive hMG/FSH be administered for a longer period than would be necessary before the woman is adequately stimulated. In spite of these drawbacks, we believe that the GnRH agonist presents a significant breakthrough in the treatment of couples who are resistant to hMG/FSH therapy.

Evaluation of Follicular Development

In order to properly schedule surgical retrieval of eggs either by laparoscopy or by ultrasound needle-aspiration, the IVF physician must be sure that proper follicular development has occurred. In vitro fertilization programs rely heavily on the woman's daily blood-estrogen levels to assess follicular development. Most IVF programs also employ ultrasound measurement of follicular dimensions in order to fine-tune the scheduling of egg retrieval. Usually by day 9 to 12 of the cycle, follicular development is evaluated and a go/no-go decision can be made about whether to proceed to egg retrieval.

The Role of Ultrasound

Ultrasound is a painless procedure that transforms high-frequency sound waves as they travel through body tissue and fluid into images on a TV-like screen. The woman can feel the pressure of the ultrasound transducer on her abdomen or in her vagina, but she cannot feel or hear the sound waves. There is no evidence that the ultrasound waves cause any significant damage to the eggs. Ultrasound enables the physician to see the woman's ovaries clearly and to identify, count, and even measure the fluid-filled follicles as they develop. As ovulation approaches, the follicles tend to get larger, and monitoring their development by ultrasound provides an important indicator of the expected time of ovulation.

Clomiphene Citrate and Combinations

All patients receiving clomiphene alone or in combination with hMG should always have follicular growth measured by ultrasound during the last few days of stimulation. There is little

doubt that the likelihood of retrieving mature eggs from a particular follicle will directly correlate with the size of each individual follicle, and this can only be monitored by repeated ultrasound assessment.

Stimulation by hMG

A traditional method of monitoring the response to hMG is by measuring the level of the hormone estrogen (the estradiol/E_2) that is secreted into the bloodstream by the growing ovarian follicles. The estradiol level gives an approximate indication of how many eggs the physician might expect to retrieve; in general, the higher the estradiol level the more eggs. This test will usually be done daily during the latter part of the treatment cycle preceding egg retrieval; in some programs the estradiol level is measured throughout the entire treatment cycle.

When pure hMG is administered (in contrast to cases when clomiphene is used alone or in combination with hMG), follicular size as measured by ultrasound has little bearing on the likelihood that the follicle will produce a healthy egg. The smallest follicles, under pure hMG stimulation, commonly produce healthy, mature eggs. Usually, each mature follicle contains at least one egg.

If a woman taking hMG does not stimulate high enough after a week or so, she can continue hMG medication for a few more days while her response is monitored by blood tests and/or ultrasound examinations. Such a delay should not significantly decrease her chance of getting pregnant. In certain cases a woman will show an optimal response to hMG followed by an unexpected drop in hormone levels prior to egg retrieval. This is usually an indication that large amounts of the hormone LH have been spontaneously released prematurely, thus threatening the health of the follicles and eggs. When this occurs the physician should consider canceling the treatment cycle and should reassess both the method and dosage of stimulation in a subsequent cycle.

The Injection of hCG—A Safety Valve

When plasma estradiol levels and/or ultrasound assessment indicate that the follicular development of a woman taking hMG is high enough to produce an adequate number of eggs but not too high to cause dangerous side effects, she will be given an injection of hCG (*human chorionic gonadotropin*) to ripen the follicles and eggs for ovulation. The hCG triggers ovulation, which occurs within 36 to 40 hours, in the same manner as does the surge of LH in nature.

Similar in structure to LH, hCG is favored for the induction of ovulation over the expensive processed LH. Human chorionic gonadotropin, the same hormone that is measured to assess whether a woman is pregnant, is derived from the urine of pregnant women. Because hCG is broken down and made inactive when it passes through the stomach if taken in pill form, it must be injected in order to be transported directly to the ovaries.

After the administration of hCG, egg retrieval surgery is scheduled to be performed within 33 to 36 hours—immediately prior to the anticipated time of ovulation. The follicles will then continue to grow until the eggs are retrieved or ovulation occurs.

The physician should consider the following two factors when judging whether to administer hCG: (1) the woman's previous response pattern to the same or similar fertility drugs, and (2) whether she has been ovulating regularly (see Chapter 8 for an explanation of how the regularity of ovulation can be determined).

We have observed that the vast majority of women who undergo IVF are usually ovulating regularly; and for reasons that cannot be easily explained, ovulating women are very unlikely to develop major side effects from fertility drugs. This knowledge enables the physician to make more informed judgments about the likelihood of side effects and, accordingly, whether hCG should be administered. And because hMG is unlikely to produce any serious side effects until the woman receives the injection of hCG, the decision to withhold hCG

provides additional protection against the hazards of overstimulation (see "Side Effects of hMG" earlier in this chapter).

Moving on to Egg Retrieval

The woman who is optimally stimulated will, in our opinion, demonstrate a continuing rise or at least maintain a sustained level of estradiol for the ensuing few days upon discontinuation of hMG or clomiphene plus hMG. This would confirm that follicles and eggs are continuing to develop toward optimal maturation. Moreover, it has been demonstrated that a drop in the estradiol level after hMG is discontinued will invariably be associated with a decline in the quality of the eggs to be retrieved. Accordingly, many programs allow the elapse of a day or two before discontinuing hMG therapy and administering hCG in order to assess whether the estradiol level will continue to rise. If the estradiol level declines, further treatment probably will be deferred until a later cycle. If, however, the estradiol level has been sustained or shows a progressive rise, the patient is eligible for egg retrieval.

The timing of egg retrieval depends on the stimulation technique used. When clomiphene is administered alone, egg retrieval is often scheduled for 27 to 28 hours after the onset of the LH surge is detected in the woman's blood. If she has been stimulated with hMG, the optimum time for egg retrieval is from 33 to 36 hours after the final hCG injection is administered.

The average number of eggs retrieved varies from program to program, depending on the method and the degree of stimulation used (the higher the hormonal levels = the more eggs can be expected). We average six to eight eggs per retrieval attempt, though we have retrieved as many as twenty-four eggs at one time.

Overcoming the induction-of-ovulation hurdle is particularly significant in an IVF program that is selective about allowing couples to progress from one step to the next. A reputable IVF program should avoid the temptation to proceed to egg retrieval just because there is a slight chance that the woman might conceive. In our opinion, unless the woman has been stimulated as well as she possibly could be, the medical team should resist all pressures to continue. As one doctor explained:

> I have sent patients back to South America and Europe when they didn't stimulate adequately because I didn't feel it was fair to attempt egg retrieval at that point. I thought they might produce more eggs and thus have a better chance of conceiving if they made another try at stimulation a few months later. I always make it clear up front that couples have to pass the stimulation hurdle before they can go on to egg retrieval.

However, couples able to negotiate the induction-of-ovulation hurdle have a right to be guardedly optimistic about their chances of success. This is how one IVF physician encourages his patients and at the same time helps them maintain realistic expectations:

> While the level of their hormones and the ultrasound findings roughly correlate with the chances of retrieving a large number of eggs, this doesn't always hold true. Sometimes the follicles don't want to give up the eggs, or scar tissue may prevent us from reaching the ovary. And just because we retrieve an egg doesn't mean it will fertilize.

> If we get a lot of eggs, that's great. But if we don't, I always emphasize that we have had pregnancies result from the transfer of just one embryo.

CHAPTER 6

IVF Step 3:
Egg Retrieval

Arrival at Step 3 represents a major accomplishment for IVF candidates because it means that the woman has been optimally prepared, both physically and emotionally, for egg retrieval. Now, for the first time in the treatment cycle she and her partner have a realistic expectation of conceiving since the IVF pregnancy rate is usually based on the chance of getting pregnant after undergoing egg retrieval. Their chance of success is the pregnancy rate quoted by the program they have selected.

The egg retrieval phase exacts the greatest physical, emotional, and financial investment the couple will be expected to make in the entire treatment cycle. From egg retrieval onwards the financial investment in IVF escalates sharply by the hour, largely because of egg retrieval, laboratory fees for fertilization, and the costs of embryo transfer. This outlay is particularly burdensome in the United States, where most couples must assume the entire expense since most insurance companies will not fund these procedures.

Laparoscopy: The First Option for Egg Retrieval

The Consultation

Prior to egg retrieval, the couple should have a refresher consultation with the physician who will actually perform the procedure. They should also meet with the rest of the IVF team who will be involved, including the nurses who will provide postoperative care.

The surgeon should give the couple a detailed explanation about laparoscopy and describe how the woman could expect to feel afterwards. In addition, the surgeon should point out that although serious complications are unlikely following laparoscopy, no one should undergo any kind of surgical procedure with the idea that there is no risk whatsoever. Although they are rare, complications following laparoscopy may include infection, bleeding, and injury to surrounding structures such as the bowel, bladder, or major blood vessels.

A similar consultation should take place with the couple's anesthesiologist, who will explain that the tube put down the woman's throat during surgery may cause her to have a sore throat when she wakes up. The anesthesiologist should also review the woman's medical history, looking for conditions that could complicate the anesthesiology or surgery. In the event that any such factors are detected, the anesthesiologist may call for an electrocardiogram, blood or urine tests, or other appropriate diagnostic measures in order to ensure that the surgery can proceed safely.

Finally—prior to the administration of premedication—the woman and her husband should be asked to decide what to do with the eggs that are retrieved. The physician should reiterate the various scenarios previously discussed during the initial consultation, including a reminder that the more embryos transferred the higher the pregnancy rate—with the concurrent risk of multiple pregnancy (see Chapter 4). The couple will usually be expected to complete and sign a directive stating how many eggs they want fertilized, how many (if any) should be frozen, how many (if any) may be donated, and any other requests for the disposition of their eggs. Finally, both partners will be asked to read and sign an informed-consent form that indicates that they understand the egg-retrieval procedure and the risks associated with it.

The Egg Retrieval

When the woman is fully anesthetized, the surgeon will usually first make an incision at or near the belly button, so a long, thin needle can be inserted into the abdomen. The needle is attached to a gas supply, with which the surgeon inflates the abdomen to push the bowel and other organs aside for improved access to the uterus and ovaries.

After the abdomen has been insufflated with gas, the needle is withdrawn and a laparoscope is inserted in its place. This long, thin telescope-like instrument is equipped with a high-intensity light source and a system of lenses, thus enabling the surgeon to actually see abdominal and pelvic structures, including the ovaries and fallopian tubes. Depending on the specific IVF program, one or two additional puncture sites might then be made above the pubic bone so instruments can be inserted to manipulate the ovaries or hold them steady to facilitate the retrieval of eggs from the follicles.

When all these instruments are in place, the surgeon inserts a double-bore needle into the woman's abdomen. Some programs, including ours, use a separate puncture site for this needle because we believe it allows for greater maneuverability of the needle. Others insert the needle through a groove or sleeve located alongside a modified laparoscope known as an *operating laparoscope*. Either method is acceptable.

The surgeon then inserts the double-bore needle into a mature follicle, sucks the follicular fluid out through one of the needle's canals, and places the fluid in a test tube. The emptied follicle then collapses like a deflated balloon. The physician immediately reinflates the follicle by injecting a salt solution through the needle's second canal, and then aspirates that solution and places it in the test tube. (The solution probably will contain the anticoagulant heparin, which temporarily prevents the blood from clotting and thus inhibiting the suction procedure.)

After the test tube has been carefully labeled, it is rushed to the laboratory, where the flushings are immediately examined to determine if an egg was retrieved. This process is repeated over and over until the laboratory staff report that they have detected an egg in the follicular flushings. Many programs will also have the egg graded according to quality, which provides an indication of the likelihood that it will fertilize. In most cases the surgeon waits for the laboratory to examine the fluid and confirm that an egg was retrieved before proceeding to another follicle. The surgeon then progresses from one follicle to another, repeating the same procedure until all or most of the follicles have been aspirated from both ovaries and until as many eggs as possible have been retrieved.

By the time that all or most of the follicles have been aspirated, some of the follicular fluid and flushings will have pooled in the abdominal cavity. The physician will also retrieve this residual fluid and send it to the laboratory to maximize the number of eggs retrieved.

The laparoscopy usually takes up to an hour. Immediately afterwards the surgeon will inform the male partner as to how many eggs were retrieved. When the woman wakes up and is coherent (about 30 minutes after surgery) the man usually will be invited into the recovery room to discuss the results with her. (The woman can expect to spend between two and five hours in the recovery room.)

As the woman will have been told beforehand by the physician and/or nurse-coordinator, the gas used to inflate the abdomen may become trapped above the liver under the diaphragm and can irritate the phrenic nerve; this produces pain in the right shoulder, right arm, and neck that might persist for 24 to 36 hours. She may also feel abdominal gas pains, and will experience discomfort from the incisions in the abdomen for 24 to 48 hours and sometimes even longer.

Prior to her release from the recovery room, the woman is given instructions about postoperative care, including methods of relieving any discomfort. She should be advised to use only nonaspirin pain relievers, to restrict her diet to light meals for the next day or two, and to notify the IVF clinic or surgeon immediately if she experiences symptoms such as severe bleeding. She should take her temperature twice daily and notify the clinic if it remains elevated over 100°F for longer than 12 hours. In addition, the couple should probably be asked to refrain from sexual intercourse for the next few days.

As mentioned earlier, women who receive fertility drugs very often have corpus-luteum insufficiency. For this reason, from the day of egg retrieval onwards, many programs administer injections or vaginal suppositories containing progesterone to augment the production of progesterone by the corpus luteum.

Ultrasound: The Second Option for Egg Retrieval

The Consultation

Unlike laparoscopy, which must be performed in a fully equipped operating room, egg retrieval under guidance by ultrasound can be done in a doctor's office in a specially equipped room. (It is not necessarily required that an anesthesiologist be present for ultrasonic egg retrieval.)

During the consultation the physician will explain that the woman probably will be given sedation and pain medication intravenously to put her into a "twilight sleep" before and during the procedure. The woman will be told that under such circumstances she might possibly be aware of what is being done and might experience some discomfort, although in most cases she should not feel any pain. If this does not suffice the woman may require a light general anesthetic. She can also be told to expect little if any discomfort afterwards.

Again, prior to the administration of any medication, the physician and couple will discuss the disposition of the eggs that are retrieved, and they will be asked to complete and sign the appropriate forms and releases.

The Egg Retrieval

If the ultrasound procedure is to be done through the vagina, as is usually the case, the physician will introduce a long sterile probe into the vagina. The probe is the projector that transmits the clearly identifiable image of each ovarian follicle to the ultrasound viewing monitor. The physician will then pass a double-bore needle via a sleeve alongside the probe through the top of the woman's vagina into the ovarian follicles. (In some cases a local anesthetic may be applied to the upper part of the vagina before the needle is introduced.)

The physician should be able to accurately direct the needle into the follicles by visualizing its progress on the ultrasound screen. Then, as with laparoscopy, the aspiration-flushing-aspiration process would be repeated with each follicle in turn until the laboratory reports the retrieval of an egg in each case. Should any eggs fall out of the ovary into the abdominal cavity it is unlikely that they could be retrieved because, in contrast to laparoscopy, the physician cannot see into the cavity and therefore cannot retrieve any pooled blood and/or eggs.

When ultrasound-directed egg retrieval is done through the abdominal wall rather than through the vagina, the woman is required to fill her bladder prior to the procedure so the bladder can push the ovaries into a more accessible position. The physician then passes the needle through the abdominal wall and the bladder into the follicles. This approach has been largely surpassed by the transvaginal procedure, however.

On rare occasions the needle is passed through the urethra (the opening through which urine passes from the bladder) and the bladder wall into the ovaries; this is known as a transurethral egg retrieval. This procedure has likewise been largely replaced by the transvaginal approach.

Immediately following the procedure the woman and her partner are informed as to the number and quality of eggs that have been retrieved. Because most of these ultrasound-guided procedures are mostly done under sedation rather than general anesthesia, the woman will usually not be required to significantly restrict her activity afterwards.

Comparing Laparoscopic and Ultrasound-Guided Egg Retrieval

At one time laparoscopy was viewed as the least invasive of all gynecological surgeries, including egg retrieval. Today, sophisticated ultrasound techniques are even less invasive. Ultrasound-guided needle-aspiration through the vagina will probably transform IVF into a procedure that can be done in a doctor's office as technology and expertise develop, but at this point it is restricted to selected centers in this country.

At the present time more and more IVF programs in the United States are electing to retrieve eggs transvaginally under ultrasound guidance. Most of the rest limit the use of ultrasound to those cases in which laparoscopic access to the ovaries would be difficult, or where adhesions or scarring in the abdominal cavity might cause laparoscopy to be relatively dangerous (for example, where there is the risk of damaging an attached or immobilized bowel with an instrument).

Advantages of Ultrasound-Guided Egg Retrieval

1. Because this procedure can be done under sedation instead of surgically under general anesthesia, it results in virtually no significant discomfort or subsequent incapacitation to the woman.

2. Ultrasound-guided needle-aspiration can be performed in a specially equipped doctor's office rather than a hospital operating room.

3. Theoretically, since the expense of an operating room is often not incurred and the procedure can be performed relatively rapidly, it could lower the overall cost of an IVF treatment cycle.

Advantages of Laparoscopic Egg Retrieval

1. Because the laparoscope provides direct vision into the abdominal cavity, laparoscopic egg retrieval gives the surgeon an opportunity to evaluate the anatomical integrity of the pelvis. This enables the surgeon to determine whether the woman's infertility is amenable to surgical correction, an assessment that might help the couple avoid unnecessary procedures in the future. At the same time, their out-of-pocket cost for infertility treatment could be reduced because the laparoscopy would frequently be eligible for insurance reimbursement since it was performed primarily for diagnostic purposes.

2. Laparoscopic egg retrieval also affords the physician an opportunity to perform GIFT, which in many centers such as ours is performed in conjunction with IVF (see Chapter 11). Ultrasound-guided egg retrieval, on the other hand, currently precludes this option because it does not enable the physician to deposit eggs and sperm directly into the fallopian tubes.

3. During laparoscopic egg retrieval it is possible to sur- gically correct certain anatomical defects that contrib- ute to the woman's inability to conceive. Accordingly, laparoscopic egg retrieval may offer a therapeutic ben- efit as well as a means of treatment for infertility.

The use of ultrasound offers significant advantages from a discomfort point of view, and now many programs are begin- ning to report the same pregnancy rate by both forms of egg retrieval. Many programs now perform transvaginal ultra- sound egg retrievals in preference to laparoscopy because the ultrasound procedure is less expensive and less traumatic to the patient. But the use of ultrasound-guided egg retrieval still does not reduce the overall cost of IVF enough to make the procedure affordable to most couples in the United States. When the American insurance climate changes and more com- panies begin to reimburse their policyholders for IVF, ultra- sound-guided needle-aspiration may become the preferred method for egg retrieval in the United States.

Obtaining a Specimen of Semen to Fertilize the Eggs

The laboratory will need a semen specimen for fertilization within four to six hours after egg retrieval. Although most men are able to produce a masturbation specimen upon demand, some may be unable to produce a specimen under the stress of the situation. If it is thought that this might happen, a backup specimen could be collected well in advance and frozen in liq- uid nitrogen.

The advantage of collecting a specimen prior to egg re- trieval is that the woman can assist her partner by creating circumstances in which he is more likely to be successful. In cases where obtaining a specimen by masturbation is difficult or inappropriate for religious or other reasons, the man can use a special condom while having intercourse, and the specimen can be retrieved from the condom.

Although it has been suggested that frozen sperm usually fertilize eggs as well as a fresh specimen would, we have found that a fresh specimen is better, especially in cases of male subfertility. Therefore, we recommend that even if the man has a frozen semen specimen available, he should attempt to produce a fresh specimen around the time when his partner's eggs are to be fertilized.

If the man has very poor sperm quality, it may be necessary for him to produce several daily specimens so they can be concentrated and frozen in case he cannot produce an adequate specimen on the day of egg retrieval. In such cases it may also be advisable to enhance the quality of the sperm to improve their fertilizing capacity prior to capacitation in the IVF laboratory (see Chapter 11).

The Laboratory's Role in IVF

The IVF laboratory acts as a temporary womb that supports the delicate gametes (eggs and sperm) and nurtures the newly formed embryos until they are transferred to the woman's uterus.

Nurturing the Eggs and Embryos

Even though the egg is the largest cell in the body, it is too small to be seen in the follicular flushings without a microscope. However, it is usually embedded in the collection of cells known as the cumulus mass, or corona radiata, which can be seen by the naked eye (see Chapter 2).

Once the cumulus mass is identified in the follicular flushings, it is examined under the microscope to verify that it contains an egg. Then the egg is graded for maturity on the basis of the appearance of its nuclear material and the arrangement of the surrounding corona radiata and cumulus mass. Eggs that are judged to be immature will be incubated in a special medium until they are mature enough to be fertilized.

When the egg has reached optimal maturity the entire cumulus mass is placed in a petri dish in a nourishing liquid called an insemination medium. The *insemination medium* is a liquid environment that bathes and nourishes the eggs and embryos just as the woman's body fluids nurtures them in her reproductive tract. It may contain blood obtained from the woman, from a donor, or from the obstetric ward of a local hospital (umbilical-cord blood). Each dish is carefully labeled with the couple's name, number, and perhaps even a colored label to guard against any mixup.

The insemination medium also contains baking soda (sodium bicarbonate), which maintains the acid-alkaline balance of the medium at exactly the same level as that found in the body. Without sodium bicarbonate the pH level would fluctuate because, as any other living cell, eggs and embryos convert oxygen, water, and food into waste products and excrete the waste into the surrounding environment. The sodium bicarbonate neutralizes these acidic or alkaline wastes so they do not threaten the well-being of the eggs and embryos.

Because sodium bicarbonate cannot perform this vital function without an adequate supply of carbon dioxide, the eggs and embryos are kept inside an incubator whose air supply contains a constant 5 percent carbon dioxide. Under these conditions the sodium bicarbonate combines with the carbon dioxide to produce the chemical reaction that maintains the proper pH level in the insemination medium.

The eggs and embryos remain inside the incubator for the entire time they are in the laboratory except for brief periods (no longer than two minutes) when they are removed to be inseminated, changed to a new medium, or prepared for transfer to the uterus.

Sperm "Washing" and Capacitation

Before the eggs can be inseminated the sperm must be *washed* and capacitated in the laboratory so they will have the capacity to fertilize the egg. As explained in Chapter 2, capacitation involves alteration of the plasma membrane covering the acrosome on the head of the sperm to expose the enzymes that will digest their way through the cumulus mass to penetrate the egg. Natural capacitation is performed by the fluids in the woman's reproductive tract, especially the cervical mucus. In the laboratory, capacitation is accomplished by washing and incubating the sperm for about an hour.

The male partner's semen specimen is washed by processing it in a centrifuge to separate the sperm from the seminal fluid. The sperm gravitate to the bottom of the container, and the seminal plasma is poured off and discarded. A special physiological salt solution is then added to the sperm, which are recentrifuged until they again collect at the bottom of the container; the used medium is discarded, and the process is repeated until almost pure sperm remain. Finally, a new medium is added, and the washed and capacitated sperm are placed in the incubator.

Insemination

During *insemination,* the embryologist adds a drop or two of the medium containing capacitated sperm to the petri dish containing the egg. The egg, now surrounded by about 50,000 swimming sperm (the number contained in just two drops of fluid) is returned to the incubator and is left undisturbed until the following morning. Fertilization, the actual entry of the sperm into the egg, normally occurs within the first few hours after insemination.

The Fertilized Egg

The following morning (about 24 hours after egg retrieval), the embryologist transfers each inseminated egg to a new *growth medium* in order to promote its development and encourage cell division if fertilization has occurred. The inseminated egg in its new medium is placed back in the incubator until the following morning.

At this point a fertilized egg (or zygote as it is now called) will not begin to divide for several more hours. Once the zygote divides, it is known as an embryo. The process of cell division is called *cleavage*.

In the most ideal circumstances about 70 to 80 percent of the inseminated eggs will fertilize. However, if most or all of the eggs fail to fertilize, one might suspect the existence of a previously undiagnosed fertility problem. This is an example of the dual role—both fertilizing and diagnostic applications—that IVF fulfills.

At 24 to 48 hours after egg retrieval, depending on the program, the embryos enter the final stage of their stay in the laboratory. By this time the corona radiata cells have condensed around the egg, covering its entire surface and preventing the embryologist from determining if the egg has been fertilized and has begun to divide. In the body, the corona radiata cells are eroded away as the embryo passes through the fallopian tube on its way to the uterus. In the laboratory, the corona radiata must be skillfully removed, or "peeled," to avoid damaging the delicate embryo. *Peeling* is achieved by sucking the embryo and its attached corona into a double-needle syringe or glass pipette and then flushing the embryo out through the syringe's narrow canal, thus separating it from the corona.

Laboratory personnel often share in the excitement at this stage of the fertilization process; as one usually dignified IVF laboratory director confided:

> I still get a thrill in the laboratory—even after four years—when I peel off the corona radiata and find a healthy eight-cell embryo.

After the embryo has been peeled, it is examined under the microscope. By now the cleaved embryo is a translucent, amber-colored mass of four to eight cells. If *polyspermia* (fertilization by more than one sperm) is detected, the resulting embryo will be discarded because it does not have the potential to grow into a baby. In some cases, however, it is not possible to diagnose polyspermia until later in the developmental process; and one or more polyspermic embryos might be inadvertently transferred into the woman's uterus. However, this does not cause a major risk to the patient because the polyspermic embryo, as any abnormal embryo, is highly unlikely to implant (see "Miscarriage in Early Pregnancy" in Chapter 2).

Some programs attach great importance to detecting polyspermia early on so as to avoid transferring polyspermic embryos into the uterus. In such programs, the fertilized eggs are peeled and inspected about 16 hours after insemination; and polyspermic embryos are discarded. We believe that while early peeling facilitates identification of polyspermia, it is really of little benefit and could even be harmful because of the likelihood of damaging the egg when the cumulus mass still adheres so closely to the egg's surface.

Preparing for Embryo Transfer

Once cleavage has begun, the embryo will continue to divide at regular intervals. (Embryos that divide the fastest are considered the healthiest and the most likely to implant.) Once the lead (fastest-growing) embryo reaches the four-to-eight-cell stage, the embryos may be transferred into the uterus.

Shortly before the transfer the embryos are put together in a single laboratory dish filled with growth medium. The dish is then replaced in the incubator for at least 10 minutes to facilitate optimum pH and temperature equilibrium of the medium. The laboratory staff informs the clinic coordinator that the embryos are ready for transfer, and the coordinator prepares the patient and informs the physician that a transfer is imminent.

Figure 6-1 is a flowchart that summarizes the process in the laboratory from egg retrieval to embryo transfer.

ROLE OF LABORATORY IN IVF

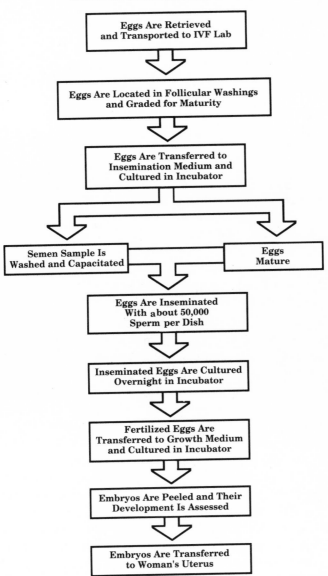

Eggs Are Retrieved
and Transported to IVF Lab

Eggs Are Located in Follicular Washings
and Graded for Maturity

Eggs Are Transferred to
Insemination Medium and
Cultured in Incubator

Semen Sample Is
Washed and Capacitated

Eggs
Mature

Eggs Are Inseminated
With about 50,000
Sperm per Dish

Inseminated Eggs Are Cultured
Overnight in Incubator

Fertilized Eggs Are
Transferred to Growth Medium
and Cultured in Incubator

Embryos Are Peeled and Their
Development Is Assessed

Embryos Are Transferred
to Woman's Uterus

FIGURE 6-1

CHAPTER 7

IVF Step 4:
Embryo Transfer

Although embryo transfer is the shortest step in an IVF procedure, and appears at first glance to be the simplest, it is really the most critical phase of the entire process. Successful completion of the previous hurdles means nothing if there is a bad transfer with bleeding, pain, and/or damage to the embryos because too much time elapsed between their removal from the incubator and transfer into the uterus. We even grade the embryo transfer on the basis of comfort, technical difficulty, and time taken to perform the procedure so the staff can gauge its success.

Embryo transfer is usually performed between 48 to 72 hours after egg retrieval, but the actual time may depend upon the state of cleavage of the most rapidly dividing embryo or embryos. As explained in Chapter 6, most programs prefer to perform embryo transfer before the leading (most developed) embryo has advanced beyond the eight-cell stage; but because the embryos develop at different rates, not all will be at the same stage of division when they are transferred.

The Pretransfer Consultation

The couple's first step on the day of embryo transfer is a discussion with the embryologist and the physician, with or without the nurse-coordinator. The discussion will include the number and quality of the embryos, how many times the embryos have cleaved, and how healthy they appear to be. The physician probably will reiterate the issues that were raised during the initial consultation in regard to the optimal number of embryos to be transferred.

Confronting the Tradeoff

This is the time when the couple will have to come to terms with the success rate vs. multiple pregnancy tradeoff. The physician might say:

> Mr. and Mrs. Babcock, all eight of your eggs have fertilized. According to the instructions you gave us before egg retrieval, we are now going to freeze four of them.

At that point the couple have the right to alter their directives as to how to dispose of their embryos. They may decide to transfer four, or six, or all of the embryos into the uterus; it is their right to change their minds. They may now have decided that the extras should be discarded instead of frozen, or perhaps could be donated to someone else (it is, however, up to the clinic to decide whether the couple are good candidates for embryo donation). Or the couple may say that the excess embryos could be made available for experimentation (although we do not do so, some clinics would use the embryos for experimentation, with the couple's consent). When the couple have made their final decision, they will complete and sign the consent forms that direct the clinic staff as to how to proceed.

Reviewing What to Expect During the Transfer

The physician should describe what the couple can expect during the procedure (the details vary widely from clinic to clinic). Some programs, particularly those affiliated with hospitals, perform the embryo transfer in an operating room or a special procedure room, whereupon the patient is wheeled out on a gurney to a holding area she occupies until discharged. Other programs prefer to perform the embryo transfer in the room where the woman will remain for the rest of her stay.

Some IVF programs allow the male partner to observe the transfer, while others require that he wait in another room. In some settings the man cannot be with the woman until she goes home, even if she has to relax for several hours after the transfer. Other programs, including ours, encourage the couple to be together from the time of completion of the transfer until the woman is released; we believe that this facilitates the bonding process.

The physician should explain that the embryos are transferred by means of a thin catheter threaded through the cervix into the uterus. In programs that have previously measured the depth of the woman's uterus, the woman should be told that the embryos will be transferred a specific depth (just short of the top of the uterus to avoid injuring the endometrium). Bleeding as a result of such an injury is particularly undesirable because it could flush the embryos out of the uterus.

The physician should explain that if the transfer is taking too long it may be necessary to send the catheter containing the embryos back to the laboratory for reincubation for about 10 minutes to restore the embryonic vitality. We believe that the best results are obtained when no more than two minutes are allowed to elapse from the time the embryos are loaded into the catheter until they are transferred into the uterus, and that the total elapsed time should never exceed three minutes. This is because the rapid metabolism of the embryos can quickly create a harmful environment within the catheter by building up unhealthy waste products. The couple should be reassured, however, that pregnancies have resulted after two and even three attempts at transfer when the embryos were properly reincubated.

Many programs consider that the position assumed by the woman during the transfer contributes heavily to the success of the procedure. Some clinics require that the woman be on her back in the *lithotomy* position during transfer regardless of whether her uterus is tipped backward or forward. Many other programs, including ours, ask that the woman assume the *knee-chest* position when the uterus is tipped forward so the force of gravity can contribute to optimal placement of the embryos.

After the Transfer

If the woman is not going to be released immediately, she should know whether she can move around freely or whether she will have to rest for a specified period after the transfer. In our program, for example, if the woman is in the lithotomy position during transfer, she continues to lie on her back for about three hours. Then she is permitted to turn over and lie on her abdomen, although she is advised to remain in bed for about four hours (not even getting up to go to the bathroom). On the other hand, if she is in the knee-chest position for the transfer she is urged to lie on her abdomen for the first three hours, after which time she is permitted to turn over on her back for the remaining one hour. The male partner or another companion is expected to remain with the patient, bringing her a bedpan when needed, food, and otherwise tending to her needs.

What the woman should expect to experience physically after embryo transfer is another important issue that should be discussed so patients do not become concerned that the transfer has failed. For example, it is not unusual to experience minor cramping or a slight discharge; this may be due to the reflux of fluid previously introduced into the vagina and used to cleanse the cervix in preparation for embryo transfer.

An Embryo's Chances of Survival

The physician should reiterate that in contrast to the 25 to 35 percent chance in nature of an individual embryo implanting after it reaches the uterus via the fallopian tube, the probability of implantation following embryo transfer is no greater than 8 to 10 percent per embryo. This difference could be due to the fact that embryos enter the uterus following embryo transfer contrary to the natural route. Moreover, embryos are transferred into the uterus following IVF much sooner (two days after egg retrieval, or "ovulation") than they would reach the uterus in the natural situation (about five days after ovulation). In addition, IVF embryos are usually transferred at the two-to-eight-cell stage of division, whereas embryos in nature usually reach their destination at about the thirty-cell stage.

In addition, evidence strongly suggests that many embryos do not survive the transfer process either because they have been damaged by an overlong stay in the catheter or because they literally get lost. For example, some embryos actually slip back into the vagina when the catheter is removed; they either get lost in the cervical canal or vagina, where they die, or slide right back out with the catheter. Some programs return the catheter to the laboratory for microscopic examination to ensure that no embryos still adhere to it, and reluctant embryos that were retrieved from the exterior of a catheter have been successfully retransferred into the uterus.

All of these factors mitigate against implantation of embryos following IVF and contribute to the need to transfer a number of embryos into the uterus in order to increase the odds of a viable pregnancy occurring.

Promising new technologies (see below) evolving for the performance of embryo transfer, might reduce the wastefulness of embryos and the relatively low implantation rate per embryo associated with current embryo-transfer procedures.

The Embryo Transfer

Immediately prior to the embryo transfer, the woman should be asked to empty her bladder; this facilitates the transfer procedure and also reduces the likelihood that she will have to urinate while she remains immobilized. She should previously have been asked to avoid coffee or tea because they are natural diuretics and may cause frequent urination. However, she might have been encouraged to eat a light breakfast in order to help combat anxiety. She also should have been asked not to take any medications, including over-the-counter drugs, without clearance from the clinic staff.

It is important that the woman be as relaxed as possible during the embryo transfer because many of the hormones that are released at the time of stress, such as adrenalin, can cause the uterus to contract. Some programs, including ours, believe that imagery helps the woman relax and feel positive about the experience, thereby reducing the stress level. In such a program the in-house psychologist, counselor, and/or the nurse-coordinator may help the woman focus on visual imagery for 15 to 20 minutes immediately prior to embryo transfer so as to enhance her relaxation. As one nurse-coordinator explained, couples may select a variety of creative images to visualize during embryo transfer:

I encourage them to visualize the uterus and the embryo growing within it. Some people imagine little embryos with suction cups on their feet—one woman imagined embryos with Velcro-covered feet. Some people like to visualize a white light coating the baby or a peaceful blue halo surrounding the embryo, or a baby blanket giving the baby a hug, or little soldiers marching into the uterus and digging foxholes in the endometrium. No matter what our counselor or I suggest, the best visualization is what the woman thinks up for herself.

And I'm continually amazed at some of the lucky charms people bring along to the transfer. I have seen them bring drawings and paintings of babies. Some patients wear fertility charms—frogs, African face-mask pendants. Some listen to positive-reinforcement tapes. Women have told me they had worn their lucky dress—and I must confess that sometimes I've worn my lucky dress, too. You can't help getting caught up in this process.

When the woman is sufficiently relaxed, she is helped into the appropriate position and made as comfortable as possible. (In programs that rely on relaxation therapy, the counselor or nurse-coordinator is usually present at the patient's bedside, coaching her in relaxation exercises during the procedure).

When the woman is in the proper position, the physician first inserts a speculum into the vagina to expose the cervix and then may clean the cervix with a solution to remove any mucus or other secretions. The physician then informs the embryology laboratory that embryo transfer is imminent and awaits the arrival of the transfer catheter loaded with the embryos.

The physician gently guides the catheter through a *cannula* (metal tube) to the outer opening of the cervix and then passes the catheter through the cervix into the uterine cavity. When the catheter is in place, the embryologist carefully injects the embryos into the uterus, and the physician slowly withdraws the catheter.

The catheter is immediately returned to the laboratory, where it is examined under the microscope to make sure that all the embryos have been deposited. Any residual embryos would be reincubated, and the transfer process would be repeated until the laboratory verifies that no more embryos remain in the catheter.

An embryo transfer procedure that includes relaxation therapy usually takes about half an hour from start to finish, although it naturally takes longer if the embryos must be reincubated prior to a second or third attempt.

One patient described the transfer she had experienced about six hours earlier with these words:

> The counselor does the relaxation technique just before the procedure because they want you to be just completely relaxed—no tenseness—just like after making love. When you conceive naturally, your body is very relaxed. They try so much to be exactly like Mother Nature. The counselor talked to me through the whole procedure: "relax, take a deep breath" and "breathe, breathe, breathe." It helped, too, because the natural tendency is to hold your breath at a time like this. Relaxation therapy really does work.

> There's really nothing to the transfer itself, not even a pinch. Lying in bed afterwards is the worst part, but I certainly can live with that.

Newer Methods of Embryo Transfer Offer Hope for the Future

Researchers have suggested the possibility that embryos may be transferred into the uterus by introducing a needle transvaginally through the uterine wall into the uterine cavity under ultrasound guidance. In contrast to the conventional method of embryo transfer, injection of embryos through the uterine wall avoids breaking the "seal" that is created by natural secretions in the cervical canal, thereby reducing the significant risk that the embryos might escape through the cervix and die.

Other novel ideas include transferring embryos into the uterus via the cervix in a capsule that dissolves rapidly within the uterus, a procedure that again would prevent the embryos from escaping from the uterine cavity. It has also been suggested that such capsules might be surgically attached to the wall of the uterus via the cervix under direct vision by *hysteroscopy* (see Chapter 8).

The Exit Interview

The exit procedure varies from program to program, but every couple is entitled to an exit interview prior to leaving the IVF clinic. An exit interview reassures and prepares patients for their return home and also provides valuable feedback to the IVF program.

During an exit interview the couple and the physician and/or nurse-coordinator discuss follow-up care, including permissible daily activity, work, travel, and when the couple can resume sexual intercourse. The woman will be advised as to whether the program recommends hormone supplementation until the pregnancy test confirms or rules out successful IVF. Some programs advocate the use of daily vaginal suppositories of hormones such as progesterone to enhance implantation; others prefer progesterone injections. Still other clinics do not prescribe any hormones after the transfer.

Some programs telephone patients after they have returned home to inquire about their emotional stability and physical well-being. The staff of such programs would likely emphasize that whether or not the procedure has been successful, they would still like to maintain contact with the couple and would be available for consultation at all times.

Follow-up after the Embryo Transfer

The Quantitative Beta hCG Blood Pregnancy Test

Eight days after the embryo transfer, the woman should have a quantitative Beta hCG blood pregnancy test, which can diagnose pregnancy even before she has missed a period. It does so by determining the presence of the hormone hCG, which is produced in minute amounts by the implanting embryo. If hCG is detected, the test is usually repeated two days later in order to see if there has been an appreciable rise in hCG since the first test. A rise (about a doubling of the initial value) usually suggests that an embryo is implanting and is a good indication of a possible pregnancy. The laboratory then notifies the IVF clinic of the test results.

Because an IVF program usually cooperates closely with the referring physician, it is customary for the clinic staff to call the referring physician with the results of the pregnancy test and ask the physician to notify the couple. Thereupon, the clinic staff may also contact the couple. Obviously, if the couple had selected the clinic directly rather than on referral, the staff would call them directly with the test results.

Sometimes the physician or nurse-coordinator will work through the referring physician to arrange for the couple's pregnancy test; the program may also forward a detailed report about the entire procedure to the referring physician. If the couple wish to make their own arrangements, they should be given detailed instructions about the necessary tests.

Hormonal Support of a Possible Pregnancy

If the two blood pregnancy tests indicate an implanting pregnancy, some programs administer supplementary progesterone for several weeks to assist the implantation process. Others, including ours, give hCG injections several times a week for several weeks until the pregnancy can be defined by ultrasound.

We believe that it could, in special circumstances, be beneficial to administer hCG prior to performing the Beta hCG test for pregnancy diagnosis in order to provide better support for the possible pregnancy. This is currently being practiced selectively in our own setting as well as in a few other IVF programs, and the results are encouraging. The problem with this approach is that administration of hCG prior to the test delays the ability to diagnose pregnancy because hCG is the very hormone that is measured to see if the woman is pregnant.

This problem could potentially be overcome, however, by using one of the emerging new techniques that can diagnose pregnancy without measuring hCG. For example, it has been shown that a hormone called *pregnancy-specific glycoprotein (SP-1)* appears in the blood only a few days later than hCG would in the case of pregnancy. It may be possible to measure SP-1, which can be assessed even in women who are taking hCG, to diagnose pregnancy while at the same time supporting the pregnancy with hCG.

In addition, some studies suggest that the measurement of SP-1 serially in early pregnancy potentially could be a reliable indicator of whether the pregnancy is likely to survive or miscarry.

Confirming a Pregnancy by Ultrasound

Although a positive Beta hCG blood pregnancy test indicates the possibility of a conception, pregnancy cannot be confirmed until it can be defined by ultrasound (see Chapter 10 for a discussion of various definitions of pregnancy). Ultrasound can then confirm the existence of a pregnancy three to four weeks after embryo transfer. The chance of miscarriage progressively decreases from this point onwards; and once the pregnancy has gone beyond the third month, the possibility of miscarriage drops to less than 3 percent.

What to Do If Spotting Occurs

After IVF the woman may experience vaginal spotting, whether or not she is pregnant. If it does, she should call her physician immediately and rest in bed. Spotting can be caused by a variety of things: one of the embryos could be burrowing into the endometrium; one could be attaching while another is detaching; the menstrual period may have begun; or the woman may have a tubal pregnancy. Although there is no way of knowing in the very early stages exactly what is causing the spotting, certain tests can help isolate the problem.

All women should take the Beta hCG pregnancy test after IVF no matter how much they bleed. One nurse-practitioner explains why:

> We had one patient who took her first pregnancy test, but since it was low she didn't take the second one. She kept spotting and spotting, and then went back to her aerobics— three hours every day! After about four weeks I called her up and asked how things were going. She said she had never really had her period but was having these pregnancy symptoms....It turned out that she had conceived in spite of everything!

Women who do not get pregnant but want to make another attempt at IVF should wait until they have had at least one full, unstimulated menstrual cycle in order to adjust themselves emotionally and give their ovaries a rest before the next procedure.

Women whose IVF pregnancy has been confirmed by symptoms and by ultrasound examination should seek prenatal care as soon as possible. Thereafter, an IVF pregnancy can be expected to progress no differently from any normally conceived pregnancy given the woman's health, age, and other circumstances.

PART III

How to Evaluate IVF as an Option

CHAPTER 8

Is IVF the Most Appropriate Option?

No couple should attempt IVF until they first ascertain that no other method of treating infertility would be more appropriate for their particular situation. Because the cause of a problem determines its solution, the couple must first identify the cause of their infertility in order to determine whether they are good candidates for IVF.

Accordingly, a physician with expertise in infertility should examine and evaluate them. The physician will perform certain baseline tests on both partners, and within a month or two should be able to diagnose the problem and prescribe treatment. (As explained in Chapter 3, infertility may be caused by either the woman or the man, or both partners may contribute to some degree.) If the cause cannot be pinpointed, the physician might recommend IVF as a means of both diagnosing and treating the infertility.

When Is the Man
Ready for IVF?

The man must be thoroughly evaluated by all possible methods before the couple resort to IVF or any other related technology.

Assessment of the Man's Sperm Function

Evaluation of male fertility revolves around assessing the quality of the sperm. The sperm's configuration, motility (ability to travel through the reproductive tract and fertilize an egg), and count (number produced in a semen specimen) can be determined under the laboratory microscope.

If the sperm initially appear to be abnormal, it should be determined if hormonal problems are the cause. This might require extensive blood testing to evaluate the function of the thyroid gland, the output of the pituitary gland, and secretion of sex hormones by the testicles into the man's blood.

On the other hand, sophisticated testing may be necessary if the problem cannot be readily identified. For example, if the configuration, motility, and count appear normal but the sperm do not move properly in a linear fashion, or if some sperm huddle together in clumps, immunologic studies on the man's blood and sperm might be necessary to determine whether his own antibodies are inhibiting sperm function. As mentioned earlier, this sometimes happens if infection or surgery have damaged the sperm ducts or testicles.

The Zona-Free Hamster-Egg Penetration Test

A relatively new technique known as the *zona-free hamster-egg penetration test* helps determine whether sperm are likely to fertilize healthy eggs. In this test, sperm are placed in contact with many hamster eggs from which the zona pellucida has previously been removed; and the number of sperm that penetrate the eggs are counted and evaluated. Failure to penetrate a sufficient percentage of eggs may indicate severe male infertility.

Hamster eggs are used because of their similarity to the human egg. Another advantage of hamster eggs is the fact that, once fertilized by sperm from a nonhamster species, they cannot develop further. In other words, although hamster eggs can be penetrated by human sperm, they will not cleave and create a viable embryo.

One of the drawbacks of the zona-free hamster-egg penetration test is that it may produce misleading results. Many women subsequently get pregnant when their partner's test results are poor; in other cases, the result will be normal although the man is severely infertile. Because this test is highly technical, with a high potential for error, various laboratories may interpret it differently, leading to the conflicting results just described.

In many cases unexplained infertility is caused because some physical-chemical, biochemical, or immunological factors within the cumulus complex prevent the sperm from undergoing the acrosome reaction (being attracted to and then penetrating the zona pellucida). The only way to determine if these inhibiting factors exist is by observing the interaction of human eggs and sperm in the petri dish during IVF.

The zona-free hamster-egg penetration test is a relatively nonspecific screening test for severe male subfertility, and a negative report should not necessarily deter a couple from attempting IVF.

Treatment of Male Infertility

Male infertility can be treated surgically to repair anatomical defects or by the administration of hormones to stimulate the testicles. Fertility hormones such as clomiphene citrate, hMG, and hCG have been used with varying success in such cases.

In rare situations, a disease outside the reproductive tract that hinders sperm production may be corrected medically or surgically. If the man is producing antibodies to his own sperm, steroids may be used to suppress this immunologic reaction (but steroid treatment itself is not without risk).

Only if the cause of the man's infertility is not correctable through minor surgery, administration of hormones, or one or more attempts at noninvasive options such as intrauterine insemination should a couple consider gamete intrafallopian transfer (GIFT), IVF, or a combination of both (see Chapter 11).

When Is the Woman Ready for IVF?

Defining the cause of a woman's infertility requires, as for the man, careful analysis of her history and a clinical examination by a fertility specialist. Three areas need to be carefully assessed: (1) the pattern of ovulation, (2) the anatomical integrity of the reproductive tract, and (3) the status of the cervical mucus.

The Pattern of Ovulation

As explained in Chapter 2, a woman is unlikely to conceive unless she ovulates at the right time in the proper hormonal environment. Reliable evidence of ovulation can only be obtained by examining the woman's ovaries through a laparoscope, by repeated ultrasound examinations around the time of presumed ovulation (to detect a collapsed follicle and/or some follicular fluid pooled in the abdominal cavity) or—the only really reliable way—by confirming a pregnancy by means of ultrasound.

It is important to remember that the purpose of assessing ovulation is not to determine whether the woman ovulated but whether she ovulated at the proper time, within the proper hormonal setting, and if the lining of the uterus is properly prepared. The following tests will provide reasonable *presumptive* evidence that the woman is ovulating and will help the physician determine how well synchronized these vital components are during the luteal phase (second half) of the menstrual cycle. These tests are valuable indicators of the appropriateness of ovulation and the hormonal environment when their results are compared and considered in combination.

The BBT Chart
One way to assess the pattern of ovulation is by compiling a daily body temperature chart. The woman does this by taking her oral temperature each morning before she gets out of bed or has anything to drink. She then enters her temperature on a *basal body temperature (BBT) chart.*

The pattern on the chart will mirror the output of the hormone progesterone by the corpus luteum in the ovary. An ovulating woman's temperature rises around the time of ovulation, and this rise will be sustained through the rest of the menstrual cycle (when the ovaries are producing hormones to prepare the endometrium). The woman's temperature goes up when progesterone is produced and stays up until its levels drop with the demise of the corpus luteum. This phenomenon occurs because progesterone acts on the biological thermostat in the brain that regulates body temperature, setting it one notch higher when progesterone is being produced and lowering it at or just before the beginning of the menstrual period. As long as the temperature is up, the presence of progesterone can be presumed.

The only reliable indicator of the exact time of ovulation or the quality of the hormonal environment is the biphasic nature of the BBT temperature—a low setting in the first half of the cycle and a higher setting in the second half. Because ovulation usually occurs 14 days before the expected menstrual period, the woman's temperature will usually be about ½° to 1° higher during the last two weeks of her cycle. A biphasic pattern such as this (the first phase is lower than the second phase) suggests ovulation. It is not important whether the increase is sudden or gradual.

Figure 8-1 illustrates how the biphasic BBT pattern is synchronized with hormone production, ovulation, and other aspects of the menstrual cycle. Estrogen levels in the blood (including estradiol, as shown in Figure 8-1) peak at the time of ovulation. This, it is believed, triggers the LH surge and to a lesser extent a synchronous rapid rise and fall in the FSH levels. The basal body temperature (BBT) begins to rise immediately after ovulation has occurred. The estrogen levels fall progressively immediately prior to, and for a few days following ovulation and rise once again, only to drop precipitously immediately prior to menstruation. Measurable amounts of progesterone first appear in the bloodstream around the time of ovulation and then rise progressively during the second half of the menstrual cycle and, as with estrogen levels, also drop sharply preceding the onset of menstruation. The follicle, which contains the developing egg and produces estrogen, begins to grow during the first half of the menstrual cycle; immediately after ovulation, it collapses and forms the corpus luteum. It is the corpus luteum that during the second half of the menstrual cycle produces both estrogen and progesterone. The corpus luteum has a natural life span of about 12 to 14 days, whereupon its failure causes the abrupt fall in estrogen and progesterone levels cited above. This results in a withdrawal of the hormonal support of the endometrium, thereby precipitating menstruation. Should pregnancy occur, the corpus luteum's survival is prolonged, estrogen and progesterone levels continue to rise, and menstruation is deferred (see "Hormones Prepare the Body for Conception," Chapter 2).

The BBT chart, therefore, (1) indicates that the woman presumably ovulated, and (2) provides a rough idea about when ovulation occurred and the length of the second half of the cycle. However, nothing more should be read into the chart. There is an old story about the woman who, after reading her BBT chart, frantically calls her husband and says, "Honey, rush on home. My temperature has just dropped and now is

THE INTERRELATIONSHIP BETWEEN HORMONAL EVENTS
AND BASAL BODY TEMPERATURE
IN THE NORMAL MENSTRUAL CYCLE

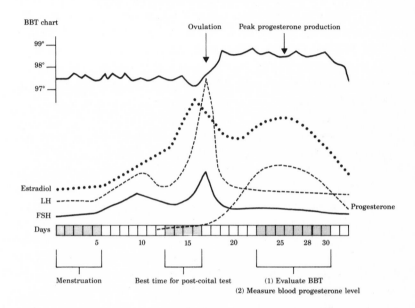

FIGURE 8-1

going to go up, so it's time to come home and have intercourse!'' She might as well wait until that evening for all the
good it would do. It is a misconception that the BBT can pre-
cisely pinpoint the ideal time for intercourse.

Regular Menstrual Periods

Regular menstrual periods associated with breast tenderness before the periods, some discomfort (cramping) during menstruation, and often mood changes preceding the onset of the periods
are all clinical indications that the woman is likely to be ovulating.

Urine Tests

Since the surge of the hormone LH triggers ovulation, detection of LH in the urine suggests that ovulation probably has occurred. The woman can easily perform this urine test at home around the time of ovulation by performing one of the commercially available "home ovulation tests" on a urine sample. The actual time of ovulation can be predicted by daily, twice daily, or even more frequent performance of the test and charting of the results. It should be kept in mind that there is a two- to four-hour lag before the urine test will reflect the surge of LH in the bloodstream (see Figure 8-1).

Endometrial Biopsy

An *endometrial biopsy,* which can be performed in a doctor's office, evaluates the condition of the lining of the uterus. In this relatively painless procedure the physician inserts a small curette or suction apparatus into the uterus and removes a sliver of the endometrium for examination under the microscope.

If the endometrium is secretory in nature, indicating the effect of progesterone, it is likely that the woman has already ovulated. A pathologist is frequently able to pinpoint almost to the day when ovulation was likely to have occured by microscopically examining the secretory endometrium.

It is also possible to determine whether the endometrial sample is appropriately developed for the stage of the menstrual cycle at which it was taken, providing yet another parameter of whether ovulation is occurring in the proper hormonal environment. It is important to remember that although estrogen is not measured in this test, progesterone can only act on a lining that has been stimulated by estrogen; so if microscopic examination shows that the endometrium development is in sync in the middle of the luteal phase, it can be assumed that estrogen stimulation was adequate as well. By combining the endometrial biopsy with measurement of blood or urine hormone levels, it is possible to further refine the evaluation of ovulation.

The LH Blood-Hormone Test

An LH blood-hormone test done several times daily around the time of presumed ovulation (at least 14 days prior to the menstrual period, or when the temperature goes up) is a relatively sophisticated indicator of likely ovulation. This is related to the fact that (as mentioned in Chapter 2) the LH surge in the middle of the cycle precedes ovulation.

When women used to undergo IVF in natural, unstimulated cycles or when they were given clomiphene citrate without hCG (which acts like an artificial surge of LH), it was necessary to measure LH by repeated blood tests. This series of tests was necessary in order to pinpoint the time of expected ovulation so the eggs could be retrieved before they were ovulated into the fallopian tube or abdominal cavity. Today, the dipstick urine tests that measure the excretion of LH (described earlier in this chapter) are accurate enough. Serial LH blood testing, which is expensive, time-consuming, and painful, has been virtually supplanted by serial urine LH testing to pinpoint ovulation.

The Progesterone Blood-Hormone Test

The most common indicator of presumed ovulation is the level of the blood hormone progesterone in the woman's blood, as measured a few days before her anticipated menstrual period. This test usually will indicate whether or not the woman is likely to have ovulated, again because progesterone is usually only present in significant amounts in the bloodstream after ovulation.

Analysis of both the LH and progesterone values measures not only whether these hormones are present but also the appropriateness of their levels in the blood relative to the time of the cycle (see Figure 8-1).

Summary

It is important to view all these tests in context together. For example, a microscopic examination of an endometrial biopsy might show that the endometrium is typical for day 25 of the cycle, the plasma progesterone level is 16 nanograms per ml (typical for that stage of the cycle), and the length of the luteal phase (as gauged from the urine dipstick test or temperature rise on the BBT chart to the onset of menstruation) was 13 to 14 days. This would indicate a good luteal phase (proper length, enough progesterone, and a histologically normal uterine lining).

The opposite situation might be—again on day 25 of the cycle—an endometrium typical of day 19, a progesterone level of 5 nanograms per ml, and a luteal phase of about nine days. This would suggest possible corpus luteum insufficiency and/or insufficient stimulation of the endometrium. In this case the luteal phase is too short, the endometrial response is inappropriate for the timing of the cycle, or the hormonal environment is inadequate. The presence of any of these parameters will lead to the diagnosis of an abnormal hormonal environment. Administration of fertility drugs such as clomiphene, hMG, and hCG will oftentimes reinstate and/or regulate the pattern of ovulation so most women with such problems can have a reasonable chance of conceiving. As a rule, ovulation problems alone do not require IVF as a solution.

Integrity of the Reproductive Tract

Since pregnancy can occur only when the reproductive system does not inhibit the passage of sperm, eggs, and embryos, an abnormality within the tract is likely to interfere with the woman's ability to conceive. Careful analysis of her medical history, including previous venereal diseases, infections following the use of an IUD, and the results of previous fertility tests, may suggest the presence of an abnormality such as damaged fallopian tubes, endometriosis, or fibroid tumors. However, defects in the reproductive system can only be confirmed through tests such as those outlined below.

Hysterosalpingogram (HSG)

The *hysterosalpingogram* tests the *patency* (absence of blockage) of the fallopian tubes and the shape of the uterus. During the HSG procedure the physician injects a radio-opaque, usually water-soluble dye into the uterus via the vagina and cervix, and traces the dye's pathway by a series of X-rays. The HSG can identify a blockage in the fallopian tubes and may also point out some obvious abnormalities inside the uterus, such as fibroid tumors, scarring, and abnormalities of uterine development such as might occur spontaneously or as a result of DES exposure during the woman's own prenatal development.

The major shortcoming of the HSG is that its usefulness is limited in assessing the interior of the uterus and fallopian tubes. In addition, it does not yield any information about the ovaries. The HSG cannot be used to diagnose fertility problems in which the insides of the fallopian tubes and uterus may appear perfectly normal although the fallopian tubes are unable to perform the vital function of retrieving the eggs from the ovaries.

Women who undergo an HSG should be aware that the procedure is relatively painful, often causing severe cramping. In addition, there is about a 2 percent risk that the dye can convert a dormant infection into a full-blown pelvic inflammation. They should also be aware that infection can be introduced if the procedure is not performed using the proper sterile technique. Finally, because non-water-soluble dyes tend to collect in damaged tubes and produce infection and complications, there has been a move away from using such dyes. However, the iodine solution in both water-soluble and non-water-soluble dyes can also cause reactions.

Laparoscopy
One way to both assess the patency of the fallopian tubes and examine the pelvic cavity is by inserting a laparoscope through a small incision in the abdomen. Similar to the lighted, telescope-like instrument used during IVF- or GIFT-related laparoscopy, it enables the physician to look inside the abdominal cavity and to perform surgery at the same time. The physician can directly visualize the patency of the fallopian tubes during laparoscopy by injecting a colored, water-soluble (non-iodine) solution into the uterus through the vagina and cervix,

and then observing the fluid's passage through the fallopian tubes. It is also possible to microscopically examine the ends of the fallopian tubes through the laparoscope.

In a new procedure known as *salpingoscopy* the physician can direct (by watching through the laparoscope) a thin fiberoptic catheter through a separate puncture site into one or both of the fallopian tubes, and then examine the tubal lining for adhesions or damage. Salpingoscopy even enables the physician to perform surgery inside the fallopian tubes through the salpingoscope, thus avoiding the need to open the abdominal cavity except for the small puncture site. During the same procedure the physician can examine the ovaries as well as the exterior of the fallopian tubes and uterus to see if endometriosis, inflammation, or any other anatomic defect might be contributing toward the woman's infertility.

Because of its ability to both assess tubal patency and enable the physician to visualize the abdominal cavity, laparoscopy has largely replaced the hysterosalpingogram as the most popular method of assessing the anatomical integrity of the reproductive tract.

We have introduced a successful procedure called *augmented laparoscopy,* or "diagnostic IVF," which offers an opportunity for the woman to attempt to conceive while being evaluated as to the cause of her infertility. This procedure might be particularly appropriate for a woman who is suspected of having tubal blockage caused by pelvic disease. First, the woman undergoes a simple procedure such as HSG to confirm whether the fallopian tubes are patent or not, and then she is stimulated with fertility drugs and scheduled for a diagnostic laparoscopy. The extent of pelvic disease is diagnosed during this procedure, and at the same time her eggs are retrieved and then fertilized in the laboratory; the resulting embryos are transferred into her uterus a few days later, as with normal IVF procedure.

We feel strongly that augmented laparoscopy should be regarded as primarily a diagnostic procedure. For example, if it is determined during the augmented laparoscopy that surgical correction of an anatomical defect would best address her fertility problem—and if she does not get pregnant that cycle—surgery rather than repeated IVF procedures should be recommended. However, many women have been able to conceive during this laparoscopic workup for infertility, thereby bypassing the subsequent need for more extensive surgery or repeated attempts at IVF.

Hysteroscopy
Hysteroscopy enables the surgeon to examine the cervical canal and the inside of the uterus under direct vision for defects that might cause infertility, such as small outgrowths or polyps, fibroid tumors, bands of scar tissue, or congenital abnormalities.

This procedure is done by inserting a lighted, telescope-like instrument known as a *hysteroscope* through the vagina and cervix into the uterus. In order to fully examine the endometrium, the uterus is first distended with a fluid or carbon dioxide gas, which is passed through a sleeve adjacent to the hysteroscope.

Surgical procedures to correct defects can be done through the hysteroscope, thereby avoiding the need for major abdominal surgery, with its incumbent risks.

This diagnostic and therapeutic procedure is usually performed in an operating room under local or general anesthesia, and it can even be done safely under sedation and local anesthesia in a doctor's office. The risks are minimal. Rarely, perforation of the uterus might occur, or bleeding may follow a surgical procedure performed through the hysteroscope.

Reparative Surgery to Correct Anatomical Defects
In most cases the physician would first attempt to correct defects in the reproductive tract by the least traumatic form of surgery, probably through the laparoscope, salpingoscope, or hysteroscope. If this is not advisable, abdominal or vaginal surgery may be necessary. For example, removal of lesions in the uterus might require major surgery in which the abdominal wall is opened.

The advisability of corrective surgery on the fallopian tubes depends on the situation. If the woman has had a previous tubal ligation for the purpose of sterilization and now wants her fallopian tubes reconnected, tubal microsurgery may be her best option, depending on whether (1) the entire tube was destroyed in the process, (2) there is enough of the tube remaining on either end to allow reconnection, (3) the fimbriated ends of the fallopian tubes are intact, and (4) previous surgery has caused scarring around the tube that inhibits normal egg pickup by the fimbriae.

In general, the forms of sterilization that can best be reversed microsurgically are those in which a small portion of the fallopian tube was either blocked or cut away at one place in the midportion of the tube. There is a 60 to 75 percent chance that the fallopian tubes can be successfully reconnected in such cases—much better odds than those now offered by IVF. In addition, restoration of tubal patency after sterilization gives the woman a permanent chance of conceiving. Therefore, this is one of the few situations in which we would recommend tubal surgery over IVF.

In our opinion, tubal surgery has a high likelihood of facilitating pregnancy only when the fimbriated ends of the fallopian tubes are normal or can be restored through surgery to a relatively normal anatomical configuration. Without functional fimbriae, only by chance would eggs be likely to find their way from the ovaries into the fallopian tubes. For example, a *salpingostomy*, an operation in which the end of a blocked fallopian tube is surgically reopened (often eliminating the fimbriae), provides relatively little hope for the infertile couple. In such cases the woman often stands a much lower chance of conceiving naturally after tubal surgery than with IVF performed in successful programs. In addition, major surgery carries with it prolonged hospitalization, the risk of complications, increased cost, lost time away from work, and incapacitation and discomfort.

A better pregnancy rate occurs after surgery to remove adhesions around the tubes (which often occur after infections following childbirth, abortion, or use of the IUD), as long as the fimbriae and the insides of the tubes are otherwise normal. In addition, conditions caused by endometriosis or an inflammation that immobilizes the fallopian tubes but does not destroy the fimbriae or the tubal lining are, under existing economic conditions, still better treated by surgery as a first attempt. In vitro fertilization would be an option should surgery fail.

IVF versus Tubal Surgery

As long as insurance companies in the United States reimburse for about 80 percent of the costs of tubal surgery but are not willing to fund IVF, most couples will find tubal surgery financially more attractive than IVF. They will continue to favor tubal surgery over IVF in cases where infertility is related to organic pelvic disease that has damaged the fallopian tubes—this in spite of the fact that even now they are probably better off with IVF as a first choice in cases where the ends, inner lining, or walls of the fallopian tubes have been severely damaged. (About one-third of all tubal surgeries are performed for these reasons today.) In the remaining two-thirds of tubal surgery cases, where removal of scarring or adhesions around and on the fallopian tubes and/or ovaries offers a 30 to 50 percent chance of subsequent conception, a single attempt at IVF is still not competitive, either financially or on the basis of expected success rates.

However, how can a procedure such as IVF, where success rates are determined on the basis of a single menstrual cycle of treatment, be compared with tubal surgery, where evaluation of the success rate per procedure requires a wait-and-see approach that often spans two or more years (more than twenty-four menstrual periods)? It is like comparing apples and oranges: tubal surgery and IVF cannot be compared on an equal footing in today's economic climate.

In order to equate the two procedures, it would be necessary to balance the success rate achieved through several attempts at IVF performed over a period of a year or two against the success rate quoted following tubal surgery over the same period of time. Three or four attempts at IVF, performed even in the average IVF setting, are likely to result in a higher success rate than any form of tubal surgery, with the possible exception of tubal reconnection following a previous sterilization. And even in such cases the *cumulative pregnancy rate* following a number of attempts at IVF is likely to provide the same success rate as can be achieved following tubal reconnection, with the added advantage that IVF would enable a woman who underwent sterilization, when she was in another relationship, an opportunity to conceive and thereafter to maintain her surgical sterility.

But the financial atmosphere surrounding IVF in the United States can be expected to change (although gradually) if current legislative and judicial trends continue (see Chapter 12). As more lawmakers and courts direct insurance carriers to fund IVF, the popularity of IVF will soon far surpass that of most forms of tubal surgery. We predict that when the financial burden is eliminated, most women would choose several attempts at IVF performed over a period of a year or two in preference to undergoing major tubal surgery, with its incumbent risks, associated pain and discomfort, and protracted period of convalescence.

As one successful IVF patient explains, the cost-benefit tradeoff was worth it:

> I went through three attempts at tubal surgery to open up my fallopian tubes. The first time I had a salpingostomy, but the tubes closed up again and the doctor did a second operation to try to reopen them. My third surgery was to break down scar tissue around my fallopian tubes, which at that time were open. This was five years ago. If I had only realized that my chances were poor from the beginning I might have considered IVF earlier. There's far less pain and discomfort with IVF than surgery, and—finally—I'm expecting my first baby in a few months.

This does not mean, however, that all major pelvic reparative surgery should be avoided regardless of the condition of the fimbriae. Severe lesions that involve the uterus, ovaries, or fallopian tubes and threaten the woman's health often require surgical correction. In such cases the emphasis should be on protecting the woman's well-being first, and then addressing her infertility.

If pelvic adhesions block laparoscopic access, egg retrieval must be performed by ultrasound-guided needle-aspiration.

Condition of the Cervical Mucus

Cervical mucus insufficiency causes about 10 percent of all infertility problems. Some of the causes of cervical mucus problems include surgery for cervical cancer, which destroys the mucus-producing glands of the cervix, and excessive freezing (cryocautery) of the cervix because of lesions, early cancer, or exposure to drugs such as DES while the woman was inside her mother's womb. In a small percentage of women who use drugs such as clomiphene to enhance fertility, the mucus dries up in the cervix and is no longer favorable to the sperm. In addition, illnesses may cause an imbalance in the physical-chemical components of the mucus, or the woman may produce and release antibodies into her cervical mucus that destroy or immobilize the sperm.

Mucus Evaluation at Ovulation
The simplest way to evaluate the cervical mucus is to examine the woman around the time of presumed ovulation. Since the ovulation tests discussed previously will help to pinpoint the expected time of ovulation, it is possible to estimate when to conduct this examination. At the appropriate time the physician inserts a speculum in the woman's vagina, retrieves some cervical mucus, and evaluates the physical-chemical properties that normally occur in the mucus at ovulation. Healthy cervical mucus should be clear, stringy (stretchy), and should dry into a fern-like pattern.

Postcoital Test (PCT) or Hühner Test
The next day, or the following month around the time of ovulation, the physician may conduct a *postcoital* test, or *Hühner test*, to assess the interaction of the mucus and sperm. The woman

will be expected to have intercourse with her partner from 6 to 12 hours before her appointment. Then the physician will take a mucus sample from her cervical canal via a catheter and examine the mucus on a slide under the microscope.

The PCT test assesses the number of sperm in the mucus and evaluates their motility. Usually, the presence of a large number of sperm moving in a linear and purposeful fashion indicates that the mucus is healthy. It is a good screening test because it provides a rough evaluation of the quality of the sperm as well as the cervical mucus, because in order to achieve good interaction both the sperm and mucus must be healthy. Accordingly, a less favorable postcoital test does not necessarily indicate a cervical-mucus deficiency because the sperm could be at fault.

Tests of Cervical Mucus and Blood for Antibodies
If analysis of the cervical mucus at ovulation and a postcoital test are not sufficient, the physician may look for antibodies in the cervical mucus and blood. In such cases it may be necessary to culture the mucus or analyze the blood for various microorganisms that might have destroyed the cervical glands' ability to produce the proper mucus.

IVF Should Be Carefully Weighed against Other Options

For most eligible candidates, absence of insurance reimbursement makes IVF unaffordable. Accordingly, for the majority of infertile couples in the United States, IVF is merely an additional tool against extremely resistant forms of infertility for which no other option offers a chance of success. However, the infertile couple should always fully explore other technologies and procedures before seriously considering IVF. For example, we strongly believe that any noninvasive (nonsurgical) technology that is applicable to the couple's particular problem is preferable to an attempt at IVF. (See Chapter 11 for a discussion of new technologies that might be undertaken before IVF.)

Factors that should be considered when deciding between alternative procedures and IVF include: (1) the success rates of the various procedures, (2) the financial considerations, (3) the physical toll, and (4) the emotional investment. With other alternatives, especially surgical options, a woman is usually given a long-range hope: "Now that you've had your operation, let's see how you do in the next two years." If during those 24 months she does not conceive, she may come to terms with the fact that she underwent a procedure that has not made her fertile.

Coming to terms with failure in such circumstances is an easier, slower adjustment than it would be with IVF. With IVF, the time frame is compressed into one month; when a couple fail to conceive during one treatment cycle they know immediately that they have nothing to show for their efforts. The emotional impact is far greater; it is abrupt and painfully traumatic. Accordingly, couples should be sure whether other alternatives that require a lengthy period of anticipation might not be more appropriate options.

Two first-time parents in their mid-forties, who have a three-month-old IVF girl, described how repeated failures at pregnancy shaped their attitude toward IVF:

> *Husband*: When we started trying to have a baby 16 years ago there wasn't anything like IVF available. We went through all the different fertility tests, and sometimes we gave up temporarily and then decided to try again. We had a lot of disappointments.

> *Wife*: If it hadn't been for my husband I would never have tried IVF because I was so tired of being let down. But he said if you don't try you'll have nothing. It was hard emotionally to go through IVF, to relive those hopes and risk getting hurt again, but I'm so glad I did.

CHAPTER 9

Shaping Reasonable Expectations about IVF

Procreation—the ability to achieve immortality by living on through one's children—is an inalienable right as well as one of the most insatiable human needs. This strong natural urge exerts tremendous pressure on couples unable to have a baby. And the pressure to reproduce becomes even more acute as couples grow older and become more aware of their own mortality.

Although IVF offers hope to many infertile couples who until recently had no way of conceiving, it is not a panacea for every couple who want a baby. In addition, every IVF procedure exacts an emotional, physical, and financial price from both partners, and no one gets through the program without paying the toll. All couples considering IVF should learn what they can reasonably expect from it before they commit to the procedure. Once they have shaped reasonable expectations about their probable experiences, they are ready to decide whether IVF is truly for them.

What Are a Couple's Reasonable Chances of Success?

It is possible to identify, from a group of 100 couples selected at random, those most likely to conceive following IVF. As explained in Chapter 3, couples meeting all of the following epidemiological criteria have the best overall chance of success with IVF:

1. The woman is not nearing the menopause.

2. The infertility is caused by female pelvic disease.

3. The woman has a large, healthy uterus.

4. The woman has both ovaries.

5. The woman has had one or more pregnancies.

6. The man has healthy sperm.

Although these parameters may give infertile couples a general idea of their chances, they do not clearly delineate an individual couple's chance of success. We have found that the following four physiological factors, which may or may not be related to the above criteria, also influence a couple's ability to conceive:

1. **The number of cleaved, healthy-looking embryos that are transferred into the uterus.** Obviously, the more embryos transferred, the greater the likelihood of pregnancy.

2. **The absence of any complications during embryo transfer.** The transfer is done rapidly and without any complications such as bleeding.

3. **The hormonal environment in the uterus, as measured by blood-hormone levels.** There must be a specific change in the hormonal pattern before, during, and after egg retrieval to create the most favorable hormonal environment for implantation.

4. **The depth of the uterus.** The longer the uterine cavity the greater the chance that the embryos will remain in it after transfer. A woman whose uterus is from 80 to 85 mm long is most likely to be successful; success rates decline progressively for women with uterine depths of 75 to 80 mm and 70 to 75 mm, and the pregnancy rate for a woman with a uterus of less than 70 mm is very low.

These physiological factors may influence some but not all of the six epidemiological criteria. For example, if (1) four cleaved embryos are transferred; (2) the transfer is performed easily and rapidly, with no bleeding; (3) blood-hormone levels as measured before, during, and after egg retrieval show a favorable hormonal environment; and (4) the uterus is appropriately long, a woman under 40 years of age would have an optimal chance of getting pregnant (probably 25 to 30 percent)—regardless of the fact that she may never have been pregnant before and has a partner with a low sperm count. It should be kept in mind, however, that this 25 to 30 percent chance of pregnancy is computed only after the woman has passed all of the other hurdles (including induction of ovulation and egg retrieval) prior to embryo transfer.

A woman might think to herself, "I'm 41 years old, so I guess I don't have any hope of getting pregnant now." But if she has a healthy uterus; the physician retrieves six eggs; the laboratory fertilizes four embryos; and the embryos are transferred into an ideal hormonal environment, then epidemiologic criteria such as her age, her lack of previous pregnancies, and her husband's low sperm count may be partially overcome. Undoubtedly however, age plays an important role in determining outcome following IVF. All other factors being equal, women over the age of 40 years should expect about one half the statistical chance of conceiving following IVF as compared to women under the age of 40. In addition, some of the criteria that mitigate against success will disappear when the couple cross a particular IVF hurdle (for example, a woman who stimulates successfully and from whom a number of eggs are retrieved no longer has to worry about her damaged ovaries).

Therefore, couples who are contemplating IVF should initially base their reasonable expectations for success on the six epidemiological criteria, and then should temper their expectations with the realization that many of those factors can be partially overcome in the individual situation. However, it is not always possible to overcome deficiencies in the epidemiological criteria (for example, embryos may never be able to implant into a severely damaged uterus). Each couple and their physician, then, must weigh these two sets of criteria against each other, given their own unique set of circumstances and the environment of the IVF program they have selected, to determine their own reasonable expectations of getting pregnant.

The Couple Must Be Sure They Are Trying to Conceive for the Right Reasons

Both partners owe it to themselves, each other, and their unborn child to examine what they expect to achieve from parenthood and what they are willing to contribute before they get on the IVF roller-coaster. Successful parenting is rooted in a stable relationship and a sincere desire for children. An infertile couple who embark on IVF without first considering their motivation can end up with problems that are even worse than the infertility problem that brought them into IVF in the first place.

The addition of a baby to a troubled relationship will compound the problems that already exist as well as create new ones.

Some childless couples get caught up in the pursuit of getting pregnant because they have an idealized picture of what it would be like to have a baby. They are so intent on proving they can conceive that they lose sight of how their lives will change when a baby becomes part of the family. They may not fully consider whether they are willing to adapt their life-style to accommodate a child's demands on their time, energy, mobility, and financial situation—from babyhood through college.

The couple must be sure they are not trying to get pregnant to please someone else—a mother who has always wanted a grandchild, for example. Each partner should feel comfortable knowing that it is okay not to have children at all if either or both prefer to be child-free. Granted, it is often difficult to come to terms with family and societal pressures, but it can be done.

But when a couple want a baby for the right reasons, the joy over the baby's birth may extend to surprising lengths. As one new IVF mother reported:

> We've had nothing but total support from our entire family. They call Caryn the "miracle baby." Friends I went to high school with have called or sent cards, and people I don't even know have sent gifts. We're very proud that we went through IVF and that she's here.

The woman's mother expressed her feelings about her daughter's IVF experience with these words:

> My daughter tried for seven years to get pregnant. I was beginning to feel I was never going to have a grandchild, and I worried through the whole nine months of her pregnancy. But IVF was marvelous for all of us. It was very exciting, very satisfying.

The woman's father, who was concerned about the procedure's effect on his daughter, was won over after the baby's birth:

My daughter had undergone tubal reconstruction and laparoscopies and so much pain that I thought if IVF failed it would be so defeating for her. I wondered if it was going to be worth it. Of course now I can see that it was well worth it. I just didn't want to see her undergo any more traumas.

The joy of a successful IVF experience can even extend beyond the family, as the new mother's best friend explained:

When you have friends who have had infertility problems for years you suffer with them. You feel guilty about the pleasure you are having from your own family every time they come to visit. So we all feel like Caryn is our baby. She's theirs, but they still have to share her because we've shared all the pain with them.

Couples who choose IVF for the right reasons are likely to reap the greatest rewards from parenthood. They are often the most committed of all parents because they are making the ultimate sacrifice to have a baby.

IVF Is an Emotional, Physical, and Financial Roller-Coaster Ride

The biggest decision an infertile couple will ever make in regard to IVF is whether or not they really want to become parents. Once they agree that they are committed to parenthood, they must next decide whether they are ready to deal with the emotional, physical, and financial consequences of their actions.

Both Partners Must Share in the Emotional Cost

An IVF procedure requires an enormous emotional commitment at each level of the program, whether or not IVF is successful, and this has a permanent impact on the couple's life. Because the toll can be so great, both partners must be committed to supporting each other from the very beginning.

At the present time, one out of every three women who undergo IVF gets pregnant on her first attempt; the other two do not. However, many women who fail on the first try do get pregnant after the second, third, or even fourth attempt. Therefore, it is realistic to be optimistic—guardedly, cautiously optimistic. But the couple should be realistic and prepare themselves emotionally so they are not overwhelmed by failure.

The IVF Procedure is Stressful

Both partners should be prepared to respond to a variety of emotionally stressful demands as they undergo IVF, including:

1. Dealing with general stress "baggage" (shame, guilt, anxiety, depression, anger) they bring into the program because of their longstanding battle with infertility.

2. Following new procedures; interacting with a strange and sometimes impersonal clinical staff, and perhaps with a constantly changing cast of characters.

3. Living in an unfamiliar environment: new town, different daily schedule, time-zone changes, separation from their normal support network.

4. Coping with the unpredictable emotions that the fertility drugs trigger in the woman.

5. Reacting to family and marital stress, which may be heightened by the constant need for mutual support.

6. Managing the financial aspects of the procedure.

Couples react to the demands of IVF in strikingly different ways. One expectant mother thought the stimulation phase of her second IVF treatment cycle (her first cycle had ended in an ectopic pregnancy) was the most stressful:

> One of the most difficult things I went through was the roller-coaster ride waiting for the estradiol level. Would it be high enough? Would I have enough eggs? Would I have to be on another day of hMG? It was really the most exhausting part of the entire process.

Fortunately, she produced three eggs and had two embryos transferred (as opposed to five during the first attempt), and she was five months pregnant at the time of this interview.

The mother of a one-month-old IVF son also found the waiting to be most trying:

> The expectation between each step was difficult for me. But waiting for the pregnancy test—that was the hardest part!

In contrast, the mother of IVF triplets said:

> I was at the point of giving up, and then found new hope through IVF. I was so excited—exhilarated—through the whole process that the time just flew by.

IVF-related stress cannot be entirely avoided, but it can be mitigated by a staff that helps "normalize" or demystify the experience as much as possible. The creation of an environment where all the couples are "like me" can be encouraging to the anxious IVF couple. In addition, the opportunity to talk with other couples undergoing the procedure or with representatives of a support group may be helpful. Finally, the services of an in-house psychologist can be particularly helpful.

A Realistic Attitude toward Stimulation

Couples should understand that they may not be able to complete an IVF treatment cycle on their first attempt, and should not be unduly disappointed if the woman does not stimulate adequately. One IVF physician said that he painstakingly emphasizes the fact that couples can try again if the fertility drugs do not produce optimal stimulation:

> We look upon the need to discontinue treatment because of inadequate stimulation as a *deferment* rather than a *failure*. The couple have to be made aware right from the start that they have about a 20 percent chance of responding inadequately to the hMG the first time. But it is likely that they will respond in a subsequent cycle to an adjusted dosage, so they shouldn't worry.

A Realistic Attitude toward Miscarriage

It is important to remember that the miscarriage rate after in vitro is unavoidably higher than in nature because of the effect of fertility drugs on the woman's body. Fortunately, it can often be kept low with the administration of certain hormones early in the pregnancy.

Miscarriage can have a positive side, however. Painful as it is to the couple, the very fact that they conceived at all indicates that they probably will be able to do so again. It is reasonable to expect that although a successful pregnancy was not possible on the first try, the couple's overall chances of having a baby will increase on subsequent IVF attempts.

A Realistic Attitude toward Ectopic Pregnancy

Although the risk of ectopic pregnancy following IVF is only 3 to 5 percent, IVF candidates must be aware of this possibility. An ectopic pregnancy occurs when the embryo attempts to implant in a fallopian tube or elsewhere in the reproductive tract instead of the uterus. This almost always causes life-threatening internal bleeding, and the pregnancy must be surgically terminated. Ectopic pregnancies sometimes occur after IVF when the fluid in which the embryos are ejected from the catheter during embryo transfer drains into a fallopian tube, carrying the embryos with it (see "How Fertilization Occurs," Chapter 2).

A Realistic Attitude toward Success

Couples must realize that no matter how hard they try to become pregnant, they cannot control the outcome, and there is nothing they can do to influence whether they succeed or fail. When couples become so intent on trying to conceive that they lose sight of the other aspects of their relationship, one nurse-coordinator reminds her patients to "lighten up" a bit by writing prescriptions for candlelight and wine.

The father of triplets, meeting with a group of other IVF couples, commented:

> All of us have one thing in common—we've been through the highs and lows of IVF. My wife and I represent the high! But it wasn't always easy for us. I can't emphasize enough how important it is for everyone to keep their chins up through the whole procedure.

Another man, holding his one-month-old son in his arms, added:

> I would encourage everyone definitely to maintain a positive attitude. The hardest part of the whole procedure is dealing with failures. And it's inevitable that you're going to have a few failures, and after a while you just stop wanting to try because you don't want to fail again. If you could just keep it in perspective and know IVF is a trial-and-error scientific procedure and sometimes you just have to expect problems, that will help a great deal.

IVF Also Makes Physical Demands on the Couple

The physical demands of IVF range from the annoyance of hormone shots and blood tests to the discomfort of laparoscopy for the woman, and the periodic need for the man to produce a semen specimen on demand. The couple probably will have undergone a variety of diagnostic procedures to determine the reason for their infertility and thus may already be familiar with some of these demands.

Certainly when compared to tubal surgery, laparoscopy presents minor risks, discomfort, and complications. Nevertheless, it does require a two- to three-day recovery period. Even if the eggs are retrieved by ultrasound-guided aspiration through the vagina or bladder, the woman may still be somewhat incapacitated afterward. In addition, the woman may have to remain in bed for up to 24 hours after embryo transfer in order to ensure the embryos the best chance of implantation. Finally, if the couple have selected an out-of-town program, they may feel additional physical discomfort as a result of the stress of travel, including jet lag and the general disorientation caused by temporarily living in unfamiliar surroundings.

Proper emotional preparation and mutual support throughout the treatment cycle will help both partners cope more effectively with the physical demands of the procedure. However, couples who do succeed in becoming pregnant should be aware that the physical demands on the woman from that point onward will probably be no different from those experienced by all other pregnant women.

IVF Requires a Heavy Financial Commitment

Until IVF is universally funded by medical insurance, it will continue to be a program for the haves, not the have-nots in the United States. This is true even though its cost only really becomes significant when the woman is wheeled into the operating room for egg retrieval. That is when the fees for anesthesiology, the operating room, the surgery, processing and fertilizing the eggs and sperm, and transferring the embryos mount into thousands of dollars within a few days. Until the point of egg retrieval, the couple will only have to pay the relatively minimal cost of the fertility drugs, which insurance companies will oftentimes cover either partially or totally.

However, the cost of attempting to conceive is not usually limited to the IVF procedure. Many couples have learned how high the overall expenses of attempting to conceive can be. As one newly expectant IVF patient said:

> So far we've spent about $23,000 trying to get pregnant, so the IVF portion was really a minor part of the total cost. I first went through reconstructive surgery, then five or six laparoscopies. I shudder to think of the money we spent on airfare to consult with doctors in other cities—plus hotel rooms and meals—to say nothing of all the income we lost by taking so much time away from work. Had we known that my tubes were permanently blocked, we could have saved a lot of money by going directly through IVF. But out of that $23,000 our insurance company has paid about $13,000, so we have been pretty lucky financially.

Although this woman considered herself lucky to have paid "only" $10,000 out of her own pocket, a similar outlay would be prohibitive for most other couples. That is why couples contemplating IVF should first determine whether their budget can accommodate all the direct and indirect expenses that IVF entails.

A Reasonable Attitude toward Budgeting for IVF
When inquiring about the costs of a particular IVF program, the couple should always ask for written quotations that cover all the charges they will incur. This is to avoid any distressing surprises that might be caused, for example, if the program omitted a hefty charge for multiple tests from its quotation. The couple should also not be afraid to ask about items they do not understand.

In addition to the total fee quoted by the program, the couple who must travel from their locality to a program in another city should generously provide for the kinds of expenses mentioned earlier: air or ground transportation, meals, hotels, other travel expenses, allowances for lost income, even house-sitters or baby-sitters while the couple are on the road. If they plan to visit several IVF programs before selecting one, they should also provide for the expenses they will incur during their site inspections.

In most cases the couple will have to pay up front for the entire procedure. In vitro fertilization programs usually request payment in advance in order to avoid problems collecting from couples who do not get pregnant. Most programs will advise the couple how to bill the insurance company for the reimbursable components of the procedure but will not bill the company directly.

A Reasonable Attitude toward Insurance Coverage

In vitro fertilization candidates should not automatically assume their insurance will cover IVF. Reimbursement practices vary from company to company and from state to state; in general, the attitude of insurance companies in regard to IVF could be vastly improved. As one new mother said vehemently:

> We're still waiting for our insurance to pay. It's been over a year since we went through the IVF program, and they just keep making excuses. So far we've only received $380!

The father of triplets expressed his concern about the inequity of insurance companies that refuse to fund IVF but cover other surgical procedures without question:

> Through all of our infertility treatments, including artificial insemination and surgeries, the insurance companies argued and refused to pay. Then, our children were born seven weeks premature—and the hospital bill for them and my wife was $128,000! But the insurance company said that was no problem; they're going to pay the whole thing.

The financial risk for IVF is great, but the return can be priceless. That is why it is so important for each couple to be absolutely sure of their willingness and financial ability to make such an investment before they attempt IVF. Yet more and more couples are willing to make the financial commitment. Why? When asked if he and his wife had difficulty deciding whether to undergo IVF given its cost and uncertain success rate, one new IVF father responded:

> Well, when you really want children you set your priorities. We think babies are more important than fancy vacations or buying a boat. We were able to budget for IVF. But we're sorry that insurance doesn't usually cover it because a lot of people just can't spend $6000 or so to go through these procedures.

How Many Times Should a Couple Attempt IVF?

Because of the emotional, physical, and financial toll exacted by IVF, it is preferable that no one undertake a one-shot attempt. If a couple can only afford one treatment cycle, IVF is probably not the right procedure for them. After all, there is at best only one chance in three that IVF will be successful— and a tremendous letdown if it fails.

We believe it is unreasonable to undergo IVF with the attitude that "if it doesn't work the first time, we're giving up." In vitro fertilization is a gamble in even the best circumstances. But statistically speaking, a couple is likely to have better than a fifty-fifty chance of conceiving if they undergo IVF four times, as long as their gametes can fertilize and the woman has a normal uterus and proper hormonal environment.

Unfortunately, some people are destined to remain childless. In our opinion, it is rarely advisable to undergo IVF more than four times in a reputable IVF program that gets good results. After that, the time has probably come to consider other options, such as adoption. This woman, who eventually adopted a newborn boy, described her disappointment over three failed procedures:

It's very difficult to deal with. You go into any of these
procedures with the expectation that they will work. Some-
how we are raised in our society to think that it's not whether
you are going to have children, but how many do you want?
People plan today—we plan for our house, we plan for our
car, and we plan for our spouse—and assume that the children are going to come. And when they don't, it's devastating. You are basically out of control of your own body. There
is nothing that you can do to make the egg and the sperm
unite.

Couples who choose to undergo IVF should realize from
the outset that failure to become pregnant should never be considered a reflection on them as persons. They should view the
entire procedure with guarded optimism, but nevertheless must
be emotionally prepared to deal with the ever-present possibility of failure.

Couples Must Consider the Possibility of a Multiple Pregnancy

As Chapter 4 explains, the couple who are unwilling to settle
for a low pregnancy rate must be prepared for the possibility
of multiple offspring. With IVF, twins are born in about one
out of every four pregnancies, and triplets in one out of twenty.
This compares to twins once every eighty births and triplets
once every 6000 in nature. Because the incidence of larger,
more hazardous multiple pregnancies is higher with IVF, the
couple should be familiar with the concept of selective pregnancy reduction. This tradeoff between pregnancy rate and the
possibility of multiple births is one of the most important realistic expectations that couples must resolve.

Some Couples May Have Moral/Ethical/Religious Objections to IVF

While a discussion of the moral, ethical, and religious dilemmas created by IVF is not within the scope of this book, we would encourage all couples to come to terms with their concerns in this regard before entering an IVF program. No one should be excluded from an IVF program because of religion any more than because of age, color, marital status, or sexual preference; and every case should be assessed on its own merit. The couple should be willing to discuss their concerns openly with their physician; the IVF program staff; and their minister, priest, or rabbi. Sometimes, by working together, it is possible to find approaches that will satisfactorily resolve everyone's concerns.

Conclusion

Once the couple have formed their own realistic expectations about IVF and have decided to undergo the procedure, they are ready to select a program. When evaluating potential programs the couple should expect an IVF provider to meet three basic criteria: (1) the program should provide the highest quality of medical care; (2) the program should ensure that the couple will have the best possible opportunity of conceiving within the guidelines of sound medical practice; and (3) the program should deal with the couple in a manner consistent with the emotional, physical, and financial investment they will make. The following chapter explains how consumers can evaluate IVF programs on the basis of these characteristics.

CHAPTER 10

How to Find the Right
IVF Program

The infertile couple should begin their search for the right IVF program by talking with their own physician and/or local fertility support group. If there are no fertility support groups in the area, they should contact the national headquarters of one of these organizations. They may also wish to talk to couples who have already undergone IVF, as these couples tend to develop a close network and will probably be happy to share their experiences. Contacts made through such networking will likely lead to even more sources of information.

We wish to stress that no matter how strongly the couple feel that time is closing in on them, it is more important to devote a few months to diligent research than to rush arbitrarily into the most convenient program.

How Should the Success of an IVF Program Be Evaluated?

The process of selecting an IVF program is significantly different from that of choosing a gynecologist, whose credentials alone assure the couple of his or her competence and expertise. First, there is no accrediting agency that provides information to consumers about an IVF program's competence and success.

The infertile couple should not evaluate only the expertise of one person; they should also take into account the success rate of all the individuals who operate as a team. This is the classic example of a chain being as strong as its weakest link. For example, a laboratory that is not very successful at fertilization would be a drawback in a program that has a friendly, supportive staff and otherwise presents a reliable, innovative image.

How does one gauge success of an IVF program? In the broadest terms an IVF program's success can be measured by its:

1. **Results**—a track record that is consistent with currently accepted rates for successful IVF procedures;

2. **Caring**—the degree to which the couple perceive an attitude of caring manifested by the staff;

3. **Staff Interaction**—whether there seems to be open, harmonious interaction among the staff involved in the program, and whether the couple feel comfortable dealing with the staff; and

4. **Reputation**—how the program is regarded by those who have undergone IVF, the community in which it is situated, other physicians; and its financial stability.

The only basis for judgment the couple will have when selecting the most appropriate IVF program is their observation of the way the program operates—from initial contact until patient discharge. In order to properly research individual IVF programs, they will first have to learn to understand and interpret the terms and statistics they probably will encounter.

How Is Pregnancy Defined?

The word *pregnancy* often means different things to different people. For example, the terms *chemical pregnancy* and *clinical pregnancy* are frequently used interchangeably although they have completely different meanings. It's necessary to understand both of these definitions in order to avoid misinterpreting the statistics that may be quoted.

Chemical Pregnancy

Chemical pregnancy refers to biochemical evidence of a *possible* developing pregnancy. A positive blood or urine pregnancy test confirms a chemical pregnancy provided that the woman has not received the hormone hCG recently and does not have a tumor that releases hCG into her blood (see Chapter 7 for a discussion of the quantitative Beta hCG blood pregnancy test).

Clinical Pregnancy

This is a pregnancy that is *confirmed* rather than *presumed,* as is a chemical pregnancy. A pregnancy can be confirmed when evidence of gestation either in the uterus or fallopian tube is detected by ultrasound, and/or when pathological evidence of placental or fetal tissue is obtained following miscarriage or surgery. A blood or urine test alone is not sufficient to confirm a clinical pregnancy.

Chemical versus Clinical Pregnancy

The couple should keep in mind that only 30 percent of all natural pregnancies survive long enough to postpone the menstrual period, thereby creating even a suspicion that the woman is pregnant. This means that most chemical pregnancies never become clinical pregnancies.

Verifying a chemical pregnancy when a woman has undergone IVF is complicated by the fact that she has almost invariably received an injection of hCG 12 to 14 days prior to the performance of the pregnancy test. Depending upon her body's absorption and excretion rates, small amounts of the hCG may still be present in her blood when the pregnancy test is performed, and could result in a false suggestion of a pregnancy.

Therefore, the term chemical pregnancy when applied to the IVF rates might mean one of three things: (1) that a true chemical pregnancy is present but will not progress to a clinical pregnancy (the most likely scenario), (2) that a chemical pregnancy is in the process of developing into a clinical pregnancy, or (3) that the result was a false indication of a chemical pregnancy caused by residual hCG.

If the terms chemical pregnancy and clinical pregnancy are used interchangeably, a quoted pregnancy rate could be falsely inflated, perhaps by as much as 100 percent, by citing the percentage of chemical pregnancies. For this reason most reputable IVF programs will not report chemical pregnancies in their statistics.

Consumers should be aware that some programs report "inclusive pregnancy rates," which are clinical and chemical pregnancy rates combined. However, since it is not always possible to determine which terms are actually being quoted when this reporting method is used, couples should not be afraid to ask the proper questions to clarify and distinguish between these two terms.

How Should a Reported Pregnancy Rate Be Interpreted?

Pregnancy Rate per Embryo-Transfer Procedure

This refers to the clinical pregnancy rate per embryo transfer performed. But quoting the pregnancy rate on the basis of embryo transfer will inflate the actual results because if no eggs are retrieved or if eggs are retrieved but do not fertilize in the laboratory, the woman accordingly does not undergo an embryo transfer. Thus her case, which actually represents a failed IVF procedure, will not be reflected in the statistics. Had her case been included in the computations, the overall rate would be somewhat lower.

Pregnancy Rate per Number of Women in the Program
Some IVF programs base their pregnancy statistics on the number of women who undergo the IVF procedure. But to report the pregnancy rate in this manner will further inflate results because this method fails to allow for women who may undergo more than one IVF procedure. If the number of patients rather than the number of egg-retrieval procedures performed is used as the statistical base, the statistics will naturally look better.

Pregnancy Rate per Attempted Egg Retrieval
We believe that the pregnancy rate quoted to consumers should be the number of clinical pregnancies that occur per attempt at egg retrieval. It makes no difference whether laparoscopy or ultrasound is used to retrieve the eggs; once the woman undergoes the operation she is having the procedure, and that should be the basis for arriving at this statistic.

The variation in statistics that these three definitions can produce is startling. Take a program that is experiencing a 20 percent rate of clinical pregnancies based on the number of egg retrievals performed. If the program instead reports clinical pregnancies on the basis of embryo transfers, their reported results would be 25 percent. Now, if they base their statistics on the number of clinical pregnancies per number of women patients, they might (depending on the number of times each patient has undergone IVF) quote a success rate of as high as 30 percent. No wonder it is so important to be able to interpret these statistics intelligently. Imagine how these rates could be manipulated even further if the program were to include chemical pregnancies in its computations!

The term *cumulative pregnancy rate* is often used to describe the overall chance of a clinical pregnancy occurring per egg retrieval or per embryo transfer following several successive procedures. *Cumulative birth rate* refers to the overall chance of a woman having one or more babies per egg retrieval or per embryo transfer following several attempts.

What Is an Acceptable Success Rate?

Birthrate per Egg Retrieval Procedure

While proper reporting of a program's pregnancy rate per egg retrieval reflects the competence of a program, the only statistic that really matters in the final analysis is the chance of a woman to have one or more healthy babies per IVF procedure.

We believe that an acceptable success rate is one that is at least as high as the average of the rates being reported at that time from all programs that have experienced a clinical pregnancy. Because the mean birthrate per egg retrieval in this country now is about 10 percent (based on statistics released by the Medical Research Institute and the Society of Assisted Reproductive Technology), it is fair to say that a program that offers a 10 percent or better chance is operating within the realm of current acceptability.

If the mean birthrate per egg retrieval of 10 percent should increase to 12 percent in the next year, then 12 percent should become the new acceptable minimum level. The birthrate per egg retrieval will not be 10 percent forever because many programs are improving. However, consumers can expect that the average success rate will increase very slowly.

Anticipated Birthrate per Egg Retrieval Procedure

Because it might take a long time for an IVF program to establish a high success rate based on the number of live babies born, it would be reasonable for a relatively new program to report the anticipated birthrate per egg retrieval procedure performed. This could be defined as the number of clinical pregnancies per egg retrieval that have progressed beyond the twelfth week of gestation plus the number of live, healthy births that have occurred per egg retrieval. The acceptability of this statistic is based on the fact that once a pregnancy has proceeded beyond the twelfth week it is highly unlikely to miscarry spontaneously.

In order to compute a mean anticipated egg retrieval procedure for the United States, several factors must be taken into account. First, it should be kept in mind that the mean IVF clinical pregnancy rate per egg retrieval is about 15 percent. Now, if 25 percent of these pregnancies are lost through early miscarriage and another 5 percent are miscarried after the twelfth week, the probable birthrate per egg retrieval would be derived by reducing the 15 percent clinical pregnancy rate by about one third. So a guesstimate of the anticipated birthrate would be 11 or 12 percent per egg retrieval.

Therefore, when investigating a new program that can offer no other statistics, consumers should look for a probable birthrate per egg retrieval of about 11 or 12 percent. And where statistics are available a 15 percent clinical pregnancy rate per egg retrieval is the best benchmark.

If a program reports a lower rate, or if they quote figures in an ambiguous or confusing manner, or if they fail to provide evidence that the rate they are quoting is legitimate, then the infertile couple who still choose that program have done so for reasons other than a rational expectation of success.

Couples Have the Right to Expect Competent, Caring Treatment

Another barometer of an IVF clinic's success is the way their patients are treated. A reputable IVF program should help each couple establish rational expectations right from the beginning and then follow through with a professional, understanding, organized program that meets the needs of both partners.

Consumers should look for a program that says, in effect:

"We cannot guarantee that you will get pregnant, but we can promise you professionalism; the highest quality of care and expertise; a reasonable chance of getting pregnant; and that you will be dealt with all along the line with courtesy, understanding, and compassion."

Couples should look for a dedicated, committed team that is trained to deal with the emotional consequences of an IVF procedure and avoid a program that is so preoccupied with the technical side of IVF that it loses sight of the human aspects of the procedure. No couple should feel that they have to settle for a program that offers poor support and compassion because they have nowhere else to go.

The morale and enthusiasm of the staff are good indicators of the kind of treatment the couple can expect. Morale in clinics that consistently report pregnancies is likely to be higher because the staff usually feel that they are part of a successful program. One program reinforces this enthusiasm by contacting patients who have a positive pregnancy test on the speaker phone; this enables everyone on the staff to share the joy and excitement with the couple.

Consumers might want to look for a program that offers a professional counselor to deal with both partners' emotional needs. The counselor, who is pivotal to any IVF program, usually acts as a buffer between the couple and the clinical team. Counseling can help a couple become positively involved in an IVF program and can help steer them away from false hopes.

It is wise to inquire about the size of the staff and verify that the program has enough people to respond to the couple's needs at all times. No one wants to have to reschedule an egg retrieval because the doctor in an understaffed clinic was called away unexpectedly.

Care and *caring* go together in the truly successful IVF program. If the perception of caring truly indicates a successful program, then the program that elicited the following comment from this woman (who adopted a baby after her IVF pregnancy ended in miscarriage) must indeed be successful:

I don't think I'd try IVF again in the very near future because I have a six-week-old at home, but thanks to the staff I have a positive attitude and outlook about IVF and would seriously consider trying again later.

What Is the Best Way to Get Information?

The most rational approach to assessing the IVF situation is by first becoming aware of the facts and statistics, asking pertinent questions according to one's own needs, and then actually visiting the site. A reliable program should both willingly respond to questions and give the couple access to the facility.

When seeking information about a program the couple should look for staff who are willing to take the time to talk, and respond to questions frankly and openly. Some consumer-oriented staffs will even send literature about the program, copies of articles from accredited professional journals, videotapes, stories about the program from newspapers and magazines, and sometimes names of previous patients who are willing to discuss their experiences.

If the clinic does not volunteer information, the couple may have to be assertive. At a minimum, they should expect to receive literature about how the program operates. The lack of such information for potential patients is a sign of poor organization. The couple should be wary of any program that refuses to provide any information until they come into the office. If the couple feel that they have to pry answers from an evasive staff, they might want to think twice about that program.

Preliminary Information Can Be Obtained by Telephone

The only way to ferret out success rates is by talking directly to someone at the clinic. We recommend that before calling a prospective program the couple should reread "How Is Pregnancy Defined?" and "How Should a Reported Pregnancy Rate Be Interpreted?" Then they should be prepared to ask the following questions:

1. How long has your program been established?

2. How many patients have you treated?

3. How many babies have been born?

4. How many egg retrievals have you performed?

5. How many embryo transfers have you done?

6. How many clinical pregnancies per egg-retrieval procedure have you recorded?

7. What is your miscarriage rate?

8. For established programs: How many deliveries per egg-retrieval procedure have you reported (birthrate per egg retrieval procedure)?

9. For new programs: How many deliveries plus ongoing pregnancies that have proceeded beyond the twelfth week have you experienced per egg retrieval (anticipated birthrate per egg retrieval procedure)?

The anticipated birthrate statistic is helpful and fair because it allows the newer clinics to provide an idea of the probability of having a live birth after IVF is done in their setting. Some consumers might give the benefit of the doubt, at least at first, to new clinics. However, if a program has not been in existence long enough to achieve any pregnancies, the staff should be forthright enough to explain that this is why they have no other statistics to offer.

In order to form the most rational expectations about each program, the couple should attempt to learn how the prognostic indicators for IVF (see Chapters 3 and 9) might impact on their personal chance of pregnancy in each particular program.

One way to do this would be to direct the conversation to their personal situation after having obtained general statistics about the program. The couple might first offer some information about themselves, including their ages, how long they have been infertile, what has been diagnosed as the cause of their infertility, the status of the man's fertility, and previous surgeries the woman may have undergone. They should also be willing to supply other information the staff may request in order to become more familiar with the case.

Then the couple might ask:

1. In your program, what would be our chances per egg retrieval of conceiving a clinical pregnancy (confirmed by ultrasound)?

2. What would you say are our chances of actually having a baby after undergoing a single egg retrieval procedure?

After narrowing down the prospective clinics to those that responded most satisfactorily to these questions, the couple are ready for the next step—the pre-enrollment interview.

A Pre-Enrollment Interview Is Worth the Time and Expense

Just as few people would select a college without first visiting its campus, consumers also should visit each prospective program if at all possible. A program that refuses to grant a pre-enrollment interview should be dropped from further consideration.

A pre-enrollment interview will give the couple a chance to meet some of the staff and see what kind of people they will be dealing with. Is there an air of camaraderie, or do the staff seem disgruntled and unhappy? If the staff obviously regard their position as nine-to-five drudgery, the couple most likely are in the wrong place.

Is the office comfortable and attractive? Does it create a relaxed, pleasant atmosphere? Does the program provide audiovisual equipment on which patients can watch informational tapes about IVF procedures? Of course audiovisual equipment is not required in order for a woman to get pregnant, but its availability indicates that the clinic cares enough to keep both partners informed and comfortable. A program that offers such amenities in this sellers' market is one that cares for the emotional as well as physical needs of its patients.

The couple should be sure to meet the clinic coordinator during their visit because he or she is the person the couple will deal with daily. They should be sure that the coordinator is in control of the program on a daily basis and will be congenial to work with.

If it is not possible to meet the doctor during the pre-enrollment interview, the couple might investigate how the doctor is viewed outside the clinic. Does he or she get along well with people? In vitro fertilization is topical these days, and many people have strong opinions about the doctors who practice this controversial specialty. The couple may be surprised at how easy it is to get that information.

If a pre-enrollment interview cannot be arranged, other approaches can be used to gather more information about a specific program. Phone calls to previous patients will be invaluable. The chapter of a fertility support group in the program's city probably would be willing to help. The couple might even retain someone living near the clinic to conduct research for them. Perhaps the couple's own doctor knows a local physician who can provide information. The couple may even decide to arbitrarily telephone some OB-GYNs who practice in that community and ask them about the program.

While such research about a program can be helpful, in most cases nothing can really replace the information gained during a site inspection. A pre-enrollment trip is well worth the time and expense.

Consumers should expect to do a lot of homework when searching for an IVF program; and, unfortunately, we do not believe that it will get any easier in the near future. As the father of IVF triplets said:

> We have a library at home of all kinds of clippings, and virtually every book, magazine, and periodical you can imagine about IVF. My wife did a tremendous amount of research on which clinics were having the greatest success rate, what kinds of procedures were being used, what the latest technology was. Her training as a nurse certainly gave her a better handle on those strange-sounding hormones that are used as part of the process. Really, it was a matter of doing a lot of research for us before we were able to locate the right IVF program.

Helpful as it would be when selecting an IVF program, it is not necessary that every infertile couple have an R.N. in the family if they use the guidelines suggested in this chapter. When consumers know what to look for and what questions to ask, they will be prepared to make an informed choice—a decision that should always be based on rational expectations, not false hopes.

CHAPTER 11

GIFT and Other Alternatives to IVF

This chapter outlines some of the therapeutic gamete-related technologies available to the infertile couple. *Therapeutic gamete-related technologies* refer to those procedures that involve enhancement, insemination, or transfer of eggs and/or sperm (gametes) into the woman's uterus, fallopian tubes, or peritoneal cavity in the hope that *in vivo* (inside the body) fertilization and the subsequent birth of one or more healthy babies will follow. In contrast, IVF involves fertilization in the laboratory and transfer into the uterus of an embryo or embryos rather than gametes.

We will recommend when these technologies should be considered in place of IVF, when they might be undertaken in conjunction with IVF, and when IVF would be the best alternative. Again, we believe that a couple would be best advised to first consider the least invasive and/or least sophisticated gamete-therapeutic procedure that would meet their needs. For example, if they have the option of undergoing either artificial insemination or GIFT (Gamete Intrafallopian Transfer) they might be tempted to select GIFT as a shortcut. However, because GIFT involves a surgical procedure, as will be explained later in this chapter, it would be advisable for the prudent cou-

159

ple to first attempt the less traumatic artificial-insemination procedure.

Artificial Insemination

The procedures mentioned in this section are directed mostly but not exclusively to situations in which infertility is due to problems other than female organic pelvic disease. In other words, insemination is more appropriate for problems caused by defects in the sperm, cervical mucus insufficiency, or unexplained infertility than for cases where infertility is related to conditions such as tubal disease or chronic pelvic adhesions. Although IVF can also be used in cases of male subfertility, cervical mucus insufficiency, or unexplained infertility, we emphasize that couples whose infertility is attributable to those conditions might consider the following sperm-insemination alternatives before electing to undergo IVF.

Intrauterine Insemination (IUI)

Intrauterine insemination (IUI), the injection of sperm into the uterus by means of a catheter directed through the cervix, has been practiced for many years. The premise of this procedure is that sperm of poor quality can reach and fertilize the egg more easily if they are placed directly into the uterine cavity. In addition, in cases where the cervical mucus is poor or hostile to sperm, intrauterine insemination avoids these problems because it bypasses the cervix.

In the early 1960s, physicians were attempting to enhance the chances of pregnancy occurring by injecting a small quantity of raw, untreated semen (sperm plus seminal plasma) directly into the uterus at the time of expected ovulation. However, when more than 0.2 ml of semen was inseminated directly into the uterus, a serious, often life-endangering shock-like reaction often occurred. It was subsequently determined that the reason for this reaction was because the seminal plasma component of semen is rich in *prostaglandins*. When introduced directly into the uterus in large amounts, prostaglandins are capable of inducing serious and often life-endangering complications. However, the practice of restricting artificial insemination to less than 0.2 ml of semen virtually eliminated the threat. (Women are protected against this reaction during intercourse because the semen pools in the vagina, and the sperm are then safely filtered through the cervical mucus, thereby preventing seminal plasma from reaching the uterine cavity.)

It should come as no surprise to the reader that the results of intrauterine insemination with semen were dismal: capacitation was hardly likely to be initiated, and the uterus and fallopian tubes reacted defensively to the introduction of the seminal plasma (a foreign substance).

The possible explanation as to why capacitation cannot be initiated properly is because the seminal plasma contains anticapacitation factors that inhibit the entire process. Moreover, by injecting uncapacitated sperm directly into the uterus the important role that cervical mucus plays in initiating capacitation is preempted. Accordingly, any sperm that reach the awaiting egg within the fallopian tube are unlikely to have the capacity to fertilize it.

When research demonstrated that the seminal plasma rather than the sperm caused the problem, it rapidly became common practice to wash the sperm by centrifugation and suspension, thus separating them from the seminal plasma. Washing the sperm offered three advantages: (1) it eliminated the risk to the woman of a prostaglandin reaction, (2) it got rid of the antimotility factors that inhibited normal passage of sperm through the woman's reproductive tract, and (3) it did away with the anticapacitation factors in the seminal plasma that inhibit the proper initiation of sperm capacitation. Although the capacitation reaction was more likely to be initiated with washed sperm, it remained theoretically compromised because washing still did not compensate for the vital role that the cervical mucus plays in nature.

Many women, however, did get pregnant after intrauterine insemination with washed sperm; and reasonably good results were reported for selected cases of male subfertility and unexplained infertility. Why? Although it is believed that sperm must pass through the cervical mucus, the uterus, and the fallopian tubes to achieve capacitation, sperm apparently can also be capacitated, although less effectively, by coming in contact only with the secretions of the uterus and fallopian tubes.

The results of intrauterine insemination were further enhanced when it was realized that induction of ovulation through the use of fertility drugs could result in more than one egg being released at the time of ovulation (superovulation).

Then, in 1978, Sandra Allenson, a nurse-coordinator in our IVF program, suggested that in view of the fact that capacitation had to be initiated in preparation for IVF, it might be appropriate to consider initiating the capacitation reaction in sperm that are inseminated directly into the uterus. Ms. Allenson thought that this would enhance the ability of the sperm to complete the capacitation reaction in the woman's body and to fertilize the awaiting egg or eggs. The process as applied to intrauterine insemination would involve, therefore, the washing of sperm by centrifugation and separation from the seminal plasma, followed by the laboratory procedure that is necessary to initiate capacitation in IVF (see "The Laboratory's Role in IVF" in Chapter 6). Thereupon, the capacitated and washed sperm would be injected into the uterus of a woman who had previously undergone controlled ovarian hyperstimulation (COH) with hMG. A similar technique can be done without prior COH, but the odds of pregnancy are much lower because without COH superovulation cannot be anticipated.

This new approach to intrauterine insemination with COH resulted in a 37 percent pregnancy rate within three cycles of treatment in cases of male subfertility, cervical mucus insufficiency, and unexplained infertility. At the time of the writing of this book, about sixty women had conceived in our clinic by means of this procedure.

Intrauterine insemination with washed and capacitated sperm can be performed at about 20 to 25 percent the cost of an IVF procedure; moreover, intrauterine insemination is more likely than IVF to be considered reimbursable by many insurance companies. We therefore often recommend a few attempts at intrauterine insemination with washed and capacitated sperm before promoting IVF as the best possible option in cases where infertility is unrelated to female organic pelvic disease.

The recent development of new procedures capable of further enhancing sperm function as well as the in vitro capacitation process promises to improve pregnancy rates such as those reported following intrauterine insemination with washed and capacitated sperm.

Combining IUI with IVF

In selected cases (usually in older women whose reproductive potential is fast waning), we selectively suggest performing IUI at the time of egg retrieval for IVF. In this situation, the woman undergoes COH, whereupon ultrasound examinations identify the follicle(s) likely to ovulate spontaneously after COH with hMG and hCG. Ultrasound needle-guided egg retrieval is used to harvest the eggs from all other follicles about three or four hours prior to anticipated ovulation. IUI is performed at the same time. All harvested eggs are subjected to IVF and the resulting embryos are cryopreserved and designated for replacement into the woman's uterus (or into the uterus of a surrogate—if appropriate) *during a subsequent menstrual cycle*, should the woman fail to conceive as a result of IUI. Combining IUI with IVF potentially optimizes utilization of as many eggs as possible per cycle of COH, thereby increasing the options for many women who are fast approaching the end of their fertile years.

Transperitoneal Insemination

Some physicians are now injecting washed and/or capacitated sperm through a syringe directly into the woman's pelvic cavity in a procedure that we call *transperitoneal insemination* (TPI). This procedure, which was pioneered in Europe, offers great promise for the future as well as hope for many couples who have resistant infertility unrelated to female organic pelvic problems.

Transperitoneal insemination is performed at the time of expected ovulation during a stimulated menstrual cycle by injecting washed and processed sperm through the abdominal wall or through the top of the vagina into the pelvic cavity after the region has been anesthetized. Because this is the area where the ends of the fallopian tubes usually bathe, it is thought that the sperm thus might find their way directly from the cul-de-sac into the fallopian tubes—albeit in the opposite direction from that which occurs in nature—where they then might complete the capacitation reaction and fertilize one or more eggs.

Combined Intrauterine Insemination and Transperitoneal Insemination

Many programs that offer intrauterine insemination with washed sperm prefer to perform more than one insemination procedure in the hope of increasing the likelihood that sperm will reach and fertilize the egg or eggs. There appears to be an advantage to multiple inseminations in terms of optimizing chances that the sperm will make contact with one or more eggs as long as ovulation has occurred and the eggs have not yet reached the uterus. However, it is possible that if intrauterine insemination is performed when the egg or eggs have already reached the fallopian tube that they could be flushed back out into the abdominal cavity by even a small amount of sperm.

Accordingly, we have begun to combine two insemination

procedures with capacitated sperm in order to enhance the woman's chance of conceiving: intrauterine insemination and transperitoneal insemination. Intrauterine insemination is performed prior to the expected time of ovulation, and transperitoneal insemination is done after ovulation. The rationale behind this approach is that sperm are thus able to approach the egg or eggs from opposite directions: (1) from the uterus into the fallopian tubes after intrauterine insemination and (2) from the pelvic cavity into the fallopian tubes after transperitoneal insemination.

Combining these procedures potentially optimizes the chance of pregnancy but averts the likelihood that one or more eggs might be flushed into the abdominal cavity. This approach has theoretical advantages over either intrauterine or transperitoneal insemination performed alone and offers promise for the future, but it is still too early to assess the results of this dual insemination technique.

Intravaginal Insemination (IVI) with Partner's Semen

Intravaginal insemination (IVI) using partner's semen involves the injection of semen into the vagina in direct proximity to the cervix rather than into the uterus, as is the case with IUI. Intravaginal insemination is most often employed in an attempt to assist a woman with a subfertile partner to conceive naturally at the time of ovulation. However, IVI usually offers no advantage over normal ejaculation that occurs during intercourse. The only occasions when IVI might be advantageous would be for certain forms of male impotence, in which the man cannot produce semen with intercourse; in cases where a man is away for long periods and his wife wishes to be inseminated during his absence; or when a man has his semen frozen and banked in anticipation that disease or its treatment might damage his subsequent ability to produce healthy sperm. (See "Cryopreservation as an Option: Frozen versus Fresh

Semen," Chapter 12, for an explanation of why it is currently advisable to use frozen rather than fresh donor sperm.)

Artificial Insemination by Donor (AID)

Artificial insemination by donor (AID) is the most common form of insemination in which donor sperm are required because the woman's partner is infertile. Artificial insemination by donor can be done via IVI or IUI, but AID is almost always done intravaginally. The concept of intrauterine insemination (IUI) must be seen as separate from AID because IUI almost always uses sperm from the woman's partner. Intrauterine insemination using donor sperm is, however, justifiable where in addition to severe male infertility factors the abnormal physical-chemical qualities of the cervical mucus or the presence of sperm antibodies within the cervical mucus necessitate that the cervical canal be bypassed in order to avoid contact between the donor sperm and the hostile mucus.

Gamete Intrafallopian Transfer (GIFT)

In 1984, Dr. Ricardo Asch introduced a therapeutic gamete-related technique that has gained widespread popularity in the United States. It involves the injection of one or more eggs mixed with washed, capacitated, and incubated sperm directly into the fallopian tubes. Dr. Asch is believed to have devised the acronym GIFT—gamete intrafallopian transfer—in order to denote the concept that GIFT gives the gift of life.

Gamete intrafallopian transfer can be done either through laparoscopy or via a *mini-laparotomy* (a 1½ inch incision made in the abdomen above the pubic bone). The eggs are sucked out of the ovaries through the introduction of a needle into each follicle as with IVF (usually after the woman has been stimulated with fertility drugs in order to achieve superovulation). The eggs are mixed with sperm that have been previously washed and capacitated in the laboratory, and then both the eggs and sperm are loaded into a fine catheter. If GIFT is performed during laparoscopy, the surgeon injects the eggs and sperm into the fallopian tubes under direct vision through the laparoscope. In the case of mini-laparotomy, the surgeon gently delivers the ends of one or both fallopian tubes through the incision outside the abdomen, injects the sperm and eggs directly into the tubes, and then carefully returns them to the abdominal cavity before closing the abdomen.

The advantage that GIFT holds over other procedures such as intrauterine insemination and transperitoneal insemination is that GIFT ensures that the eggs and sperm arrive simultaneously at the point in the fallopian tubes where fertilization would normally occur. By placing the eggs and sperm together in the outer third of the fallopian tubes, GIFT eliminates any concern regarding the ability of the fimbrial ends of the fallopian tubes to pick up or receive the eggs at the time of ovulation. In effect, GIFT substitutes incubation in the petri dish for the body's incubation prior to fertilization.

One disadvantage of GIFT is that, unlike other gamete-related procedures such as intrauterine insemination and transperitoneal insemination, GIFT is invasive. However, research aimed at developing ultrasound technology that would enable both the aspiration of eggs and subsequent placement of the eggs with the prepared sperm directly into one or both of the fallopian tubes without necessitating an incision in the abdominal wall or general anesthesia is currently underway.

Sophisticated ultrasound equipment with good screen imaging would eliminate the need, in most cases, for invasive techniques in order to perform GIFT. For example, eggs could be retrieved from the ovaries under ultrasound guidance, and during the same procedure the physician would also be able to identify the ends of the fallopian tubes. After the eggs have been retrieved and loaded into a catheter with the sperm, the physician might then pass the catheter transvaginally through a needle into the end of the fallopian tube and inject the gametes, thereby performing GIFT without necessitating an abdominal incision. If this technology is refined, GIFT could become a relatively minor doctor's-office procedure and might offer great hope for the future with regard to the treatment of infertility unrelated to female organic pelvic disease.

In addition, the advent of hysteroscopy and/or the development of new fiber-optic technology might enable the physician to perform GIFT into the fallopian tubes via the uterus rather than through an invasive transabdominal procedure. First, an ultrasound-guided egg retrieval would be performed, and the eggs would be removed and mixed with washed and capacitated sperm. Then a thin hysteroscope or possibly a fiber-optic catheter would be passed through the vagina and the cervix under direct vision to the junction of the fallopian tubes and the uterus, whereupon an embryo-transfer catheter or the fiber-optic catheter itself might be advanced into the fallopian tube where the eggs and sperm would be deposited. This combination of transvaginal ultrasound-guided egg retrieval with directed placement of eggs and sperm might also enable GIFT to be performed as a doctor's-office procedure. This is purely experimental but is another technological possibility for the future.

Because GIFT as it is currently performed is an invasive procedure, it is also significantly more expensive than most other techniques described in this chapter. The cost of GIFT approaches that of IVF in most settings because GIFT requires almost all the same expensive components that are employed for IVF: the fertility drugs for controlled ovarian hyperstimulation, costs of monitoring the response to those drugs, laparoscopy and anesthesiology charges, operating room fees, and expenses for laboratory preparation of the sperm. GIFT's only saving over IVF is that unlike IVF it does not require the relatively costly process of fertilization in the laboratory.

Another major disadvantage is that GIFT lacks IVF's diagnostic capacity, which enables the physician to see in the laboratory whether the woman's egg can be fertilized by her partner's sperm. As explained earlier, many cases of unexplained infertility are related to the fact that the eggs are unfertilizable or the sperm are incapable of fertilizing the eggs. If GIFT is unsuccessful, the physician has no way of knowing whether the procedure failed because the eggs could not be fertilized by the sperm or whether other factors were responsible.

Accordingly, we believe that GIFT should not usually be a first choice for the treatment of infertility unrelated to female organic pelvic disease. Of course there are exceptions, such as the older woman who has to select the most efficient procedure before her biological clock precludes conception. In general, however, GIFT should be reserved for those cases where infertility unrelated to female organic pelvic disease cannot be successfully treated by less invasive therapeutic methods.

Ectopic Pregnancies with GIFT

It was initially believed that injection of the male and female gametes into the fallopian tubes during GIFT might increase the risk of tubal pregnancies. Statistics have not borne out this concern in cases in which the tubes are apparently normal in configuration and where no other pelvic disease is present.

A significant increase in the incidence of ectopic pregnancies has, however, been reported when GIFT is performed into abnormal fallopian tubes. This might occur even though tubal reconstructive surgery appears to have restored the patency as well as the outward appearance of fallopian tubes previously distorted by disease. However, although the outward appearance may suggest that the fallopian tubes are normal there is currently no well-tested method of determining whether their internal integrity has been restored. Diagnostic procedures such as hysterosalpingogram or injection of dye may reveal that the tubes are open, but such examinations by no means assess whether the inner lining of the tube has been partially damaged or if the wall of the tube might be less mobile than desired.

Undetected defects in the interior of the fallopian tubes can lead to devastating consequences from GIFT. For example, damage to the interior of a fallopian tube from disease might inhibit normal physiologic function and/or peristaltic movements; and the embryo might not be propelled toward the uterus in a timely manner. (Figure 2-9 depicts the day-by-day timeline for normal transport of the zygote and embryo through the fallopian tube to the uterus.) If nature's schedule is delayed because of sluggish peristaltic movements, the embryo might attempt to grow into the lining of the fallopian tube before it reaches the endometrium, thus forming an ectopic pregnancy.

Therefore, because ectopic pregnancies are often life-endangering, we firmly believe that GIFT should be reserved for cases in which there is no evidence of previous or existing tubal disease even though the tubes might appear to be normal or have been restored to apparent normality through surgery.

Pregnancy Rates with GIFT

The clinical pregnancy rates reported range from 15 to 40 percent with an average rate of 20 to 25 percent per GIFT procedure performed. These statistics vary from center to center and correlate with the experience that the program's physicians and staff have with GIFT as well as with the nature and severity of the infertility problem for which this procedure is employed. Gamete intrafallopian transfer is far simpler to perform than IVF because it does not require the sophisticated laboratory procedures necessary to achieve fertilization. Accordingly, more and more programs are choosing to perform GIFT rather than IVF. Because many centers are able to offer GIFT successfully but cannot achieve consistently satisfactory success rates with IVF, GIFT is justifiably favored over IVF in those settings. This practice is acceptable, in our opinion, provided that GIFT is being done only in cases in which there is no evidence of tubal disease and not merely because the fallopian tubes are open.

On the other hand, in situations where IVF can give a better or even perhaps the same success rate as GIFT, then IVF should be the first choice. Why? IVF's unique capability to determine whether fertilization can actually occur incorporates a new diagnostic dimension in cases of male subfertility or unexplained infertility.

We quote about a 20 to 25 percent clinical pregnancy rate consistently with IVF, given many of the same causes of infertility for which GIFT would be preferred in many other settings. Thus, we believe that the performance of GIFT is only justifiable in our program when it is combined with IVF in an attempt to capitalize on the advantages of both in order to produce a better pregnancy rate than that which could be achieved from either procedure alone.

When GIFT and IVF Might Be Combined

In situations where the fallopian tubes appear to be normal and there is no history of tubal surgery, and when more eggs are retrieved during laparoscopy than are thought to be needed to fertilize a sufficient number of embryos, we sometimes use one or two of the leftover eggs to perform GIFT during the laparoscopy. Thereupon, two days after the GIFT/laparoscopy, a number of embryos derived from the eggs that were allocated for IVF are then transferred into the woman's uterus in a conventional embryo-transfer procedure. We have experienced an overall clinical pregnancy rate of about 30 to 35 percent by combining IVF and GIFT (for women under 40 years of age).

When an IVF/GIFT combination is contemplated, based upon evidence that there might well be more eggs than are needed to get an optimal number of embryos for transfer, the ramifications of the procedure should be discussed in detail with the couple beforehand. The couple should come to terms with the very real possibility of a multiple pregnancy because the risk of multiple births will be increased by combining the procedures. In addition, they should be aware that the IVF/GIFT combination might incur a small additional charge for the separate capacitation of the sperm in preparation for GIFT.

The couple should discuss these issues with their physician before opting for combined IVF/GIFT to maximize their chances of pregnancy.

Before agreeing to combine GIFT with IVF, we require that the following five criteria be met: (1) the couple must understand the risk of a multiple pregnancy and must have discussed the concept of selective pregnancy reduction should quadruplets or greater multiples occur (see Chapter 4); (2) the woman must not have any obvious tubal disease, which the physician might determine from her history or might detect at the time of laparoscopy, that would increase the risk of an ectopic pregnancy; (3) the woman should have no history of reconstructive tubal surgery; (4) a sufficient number of eggs must be retrieved to optimize the woman's chance of becoming pregnant through IVF (GIFT can then be performed as a bonus); and (5) the couple must read and sign an informed-consent form.

Zygote Intrafallopian Transfer (ZIFT)

A newer option for achieving pregnancy in cases where infertility is unrelated to female organic pelvic disease involves the transfer of one or more zygotes (fertilized eggs) directly into the woman's fallopian tube(s).

As with routine IVF this procedure requires an initial egg retrieval and fertilization of the eggs in the laboratory. Thereupon the zygote(s) are loaded into a thin catheter and injected into the outer third of one or both fallopian tubes during laparoscopy or mini-laparotomy. Because ZIFT requires the performance of an invasive procedure to transfer the zygotes into the fallopian tubes, egg retrieval is usually performed through transvaginal needle-aspiration in order to avoid subjecting the woman to two invasive procedures (which would be the case if both egg retrieval and ZIFT were performed by laparoscopy).

Proponents of ZIFT argue that enabling the embryo to reach the uterus via its natural route (the fallopian tube) rather than by embryo transfer through the cervix increases the likelihood of implantation and a successful pregnancy. They contend that ZIFT would allow the embryo to reach the uterus at the appropriate stage of cleavage (about five days after transfer) and when the uterus is optimally prepared to receive it, while IVF delivers an embryo to the uterus about three days earlier than would occur in nature. Accordingly, it is argued that ZIFT is likely to be more advantageous to the older woman, for whom IVF offers a lower success rate.

Moreover, the introduction of a catheter through the cervical canal into the uterus creates the potential for the embryos to leak back out after embryo transfer, but this is unlikely to occur with ZIFT (see "An Embryo's Chances of Survival," Chapter 7).

While the potential for this new procedure appears to be great, not enough cases have yet been reported to justify its routine performance.

Other Options for Couples with Intractable Infertility

Embryo Adoption

Embryo adoption occurs when a woman receives an embryo to which she has not contributed biologically. For example, a woman who cannot produce her own eggs might choose to receive one or more eggs or embryos from another woman. In vitro fertilization could then be achieved by synchronizing the cycles of the two women with fertility drugs, retrieving eggs from the donor, fertilizing them with sperm from the infertile woman's partner or a donor, and then transferring the embryos into the infertile woman's uterus. An additional source of embryos would be couples who, finding they have more embryos than they wish to transfer after IVF, choose to donate the extras to another couple. We perform these adoptive procedures because we believe that apart from the fact that embryo adoption occurs far earlier than baby adoption, there is little difference between the two processes.

Surrogation, or "Rent-a-Womb"

The opposite of adopting eggs or embryos occurs when an infertile woman uses someone else's uterus to carry a child for her. Most commonly known as *surrogation,* this happens when a woman carries and bears a child that she intends to surrender to a couple who aspire to raise that child. Surrogation can be divided into two categories: (1) cases in which the surrogate mother contributes biologically to the offspring by providing her own eggs, or (2) when the surrogate does not contribute biologically—and therefore must undergo IVF.

When we perform IVF for surrogation, we insist that both the eggs and the sperm must come from the couple who will raise the child so that both partners contribute biologically. For example, a woman who has no uterus but does have healthy ovaries would be stimulated, and then her eggs would be retrieved and fertilized. However, the resulting embryos would be transferred into the uterus of a woman who has agreed, probably under contract, to bear the child and give it to the infertile couple. Thus, the nurturing mother is carrying the biological offspring of the father- and mother-to-be but has made no hereditary contribution whatsoever herself. By definition, therefore, the pregnancy could only have been the result of IVF.

We do not perform insemination procedures that are intended to help a surrogate become pregnant with her own eggs. We believe that such a situation would lead to overwhelming moral and ethical dilemmas about the rightful parentage of the child. The 1987 Baby M controversy in New Jersey, in which the surrogate mother contributed biologically to the child, graphically illustrates some of these problems.

In this celebrated case, the semen of William Stern, the husband in the infertile couple, was inseminated into Mary Beth Whitehead's vagina. Mrs. Whitehead, who had signed a $10,000 contract agreeing to give the baby to the Sterns, thus carried the biological offspring of Mr. Stern and herself. But when the baby was born, Mrs. Whitehead refused to relinquish her to the Sterns. After lengthy court proceedings and worldwide media coverage, a Superior Court Judge ruled that the contract between Mrs. Whitehead and Mr. Stern was legal, ordered Mr. Stern to pay the $10,000, and awarded the child to the Sterns. (Mrs. Stern subsequently adopted the baby, whom the Sterns named Melissa.) In 1988, the New Jersey Supreme Court unanimously voided the contract on the grounds that paying a woman to bear a child was contrary to public policy. However, the justices awarded custody of the baby to Mr. Stern because they felt the Sterns could provide a more stable home. They also restored Mrs. Whitehead's parental rights, which had been previously terminated, and ordered a lower court to set visiting rights. Although this ruling applies only to New Jersey, it is expected to significantly affect the manner in which individual states address the dilemma of surrogation.

Although we will only perform surrogation where it is associated with IVF and the surrogate does not contribute biologically to the offspring, we do not stand in judgment on those who will perform procedures in which the surrogate's eggs are used. Clearly, each program has to wrestle with the moral and ethical challenges raised by new infertility technology.

It is sad testimony that standards for surrogation, as well as for cryopreservation and other breakthroughs in fertility technology, have yet to be adopted (see Chapter 12). Unfortunately, until the United States faces up to these kinds of issues, more wrenching "Baby M" cases will be fought out in the courts, exacting an emotional toll from everyone concerned, and particularly from the child.

Where Do We Go from Here?

This book was based on the premise that IVF consumers (infertile couples and referring physicians) are at a great financial and informational disadvantage at the present time, and the situation is not likely to change in the near future. If it is to improve at all, everyone who has an interest in IVF in the United States—physicians and others involved in IVF programs, insurance companies, fertility support groups, legislators, and IVF consumers—must work together in a concerted effort to help get the IVF house in order.

The IVF House Must Be Put in Order

Many experts agree with us that there is a great need for the IVF community to deal with the consumer more openly. Amongst those is Gary Hodgen, Ph.D., of the Eastern Virginia Medical School at Norfolk, one of the country's leading IVF scientists.

At an international IVF conference in Reno, Nevada, Dr. Hodgen stated:

> I really believe that the public trust is the single greatest factor that has allowed the miracles of medicine to evolve in the twentieth century.... The public has allowed us a great deal of latitude to decide where we are going to go and how we are going to get there. I don't believe we have in all cases returned that respect with an equal degree of explanation and understanding, speaking to the fears and concerns of the public in general. Certainly we are not a single mind among ourselves as to the appropriate course or end point in decision-making with regard to the ethics of in vitro fertilization therapy and research.

How can the IVF medical community respond to that public trust? We believe that the first step would be to make IVF more accessible to all consumers. In vitro fertilization programs could work toward this goal by (1) cooperatively standardizing procedures so consumers can expect about the same success rates wherever they go, (2) willingly providing reliable and understandable data to consumers, and (3) working with insurance companies and legislators to make the process affordable.

Consumers Have the *Right* to Expect Minimum Standards in All Programs

Standards must be established for IVF programs in the United States, and consumers must have easy access to understandable data about success rates. In almost all other medical disciplines, consumers can safely assume that the physician who is going to perform a certain procedure has, or has access to, the required expertise. So it should be with IVF programs as well.

Consumers deserve to have similar outcomes from every IVF program in the United States. It is unacceptable that certain programs can promise a clinical pregnancy rate in excess of 20 percent per treatment cycle while others offer less than

10 percent—or have no track record at all on which to base any statistical report. Why is it that nearly half the programs in the United States have yet to report even one live birth? Is it right that a couple should pay such premium fees when they do not know what their chances are?

One way that IVF programs can meet minimum standards is by learning from and replicating proven programs. The general factors that contribute to a successful IVF program can be viewed as a triangle, with each side of the triangle representing a crucial ingredient: (1) technical expertise, (2) proven clinical and laboratory protocols and techniques, and (3) rigid quality assurance. The people who make an IVF program effective constitute the glue that holds the sides of the triangle together: commitment, teamwork, and determination are essential ingredients for the successful IVF program.

Maintenance of the structural integrity of this triangle might be compared to the interdependence between a lock and a key. Once successful relationships have been established (the IVF program functions effectively, and the key opens the lock time after time) the winning combination should not be weakened through the random institution of ill-conceived changes. In the IVF program, as in the lock-and-key relationship, there is little tolerance for deviation from a successful relationship. Just as it would be silly to unnecessarily file away at a key that fits a lock perfectly, it is also counterproductive to abandon technical expertise, proven protocols and techniques, and unwavering quality assurance. Thus, lock-and-key IVF procedures can be replicated in many sites, enabling programs that adopt these procedures to meet minimum standards.

Consumers Have the *Right* to Affordable IVF

The high cost of IVF confronts consumer, physician, and insurance company with this chicken-and-egg situation: IVF is expensive because it is a new, high-tech procedure; *however* → a greater volume of IVF consumers could lower both fixed and variable costs; *but* → few consumers can afford IVF because most insurance companies will not cover the procedure; *and* → insurance companies are reluctant to reimburse for IVF because the success rates vary so widely; *therefore* → IVF continues to be prohibitively expensive because...

What Can Be Done to Reduce the Cost of IVF?
The following statistics compiled by Dr. Hodgen reflect the 1987 distribution of couples among IVF programs worldwide:

Number of Programs Worldwide	Treatment Cycles per Year per Clinic
20	500
50	200
50	100
100	50
220 Total	

Dr. Hodgen's figures illustrate the dynamics of today's IVF market. For example, 150 out of the 220 clinics performed 100 or fewer treatment cycles per year, with two-thirds of those clinics performing only fifty cycles per year. When one considers how many couples throughout the world are potential candidates for IVF, it is clear that the number of procedures being performed barely scratches the surface of the worldwide demand.

We believe that because fewer than 20,000 procedures (out of the potential pool of over one million couples) are currently performed yearly in the United States, most of the 180 IVF programs in the United States are grossly underutilized. One-third of all the IVF procedures in the United States are probably performed in fewer than twenty programs, with the remainder being divided among the remaining clinics. Since some larger programs are doing in excess of 500 procedures a year, that means that others are performing far fewer than 100. Yet no one can gain optimal expertise by doing only twenty to thirty procedures a year; it is impossible to even develop statistics let alone confidently report statistics with such small numbers.

How, then, can programs increase their utilization rate? Most importantly, consumers must be attracted to IVF because of its reliability and quality. But merely interesting more consumers in the concept of IVF is not enough—the procedure must be made affordable, preferably through medical insurance coverage.

Insurance Coverage Is the Key to IVF Affordability

A double standard exists today with regard to insurance reimbursement for certain fertility treatments in the United States. Few insurance companies will cover IVF, although many carriers will reimburse for tubal surgery. Yet IVF may often offer a greater chance of pregnancy than tubal surgery. But until more insurance companies consider IVF to be a reimbursable procedure, this double standard will be perpetuated.

What will it take to obtain universal insurance coverage for IVF? First, before insurance companies are likely to cooperate, IVF programs must openly account for their success rates. All United States IVF programs should voluntarily submit their statistics on quality of service for review by an impartial accrediting agency. While we are not making a bid for mandatory regulation, we do advocate voluntary accreditation of IVF programs. There are strong incentives for IVF programs to participate in voluntary accreditation, including the increased likelihood for insurance reimbursement, which then would lead to greater patient volume. In turn, higher patient volume would reduce variable costs and would lower overhead by allocating fixed costs over a larger patient base, thus lowering overall costs to couples.

The second approach to obtaining insurance coverage for IVF is for government at the state or federal level to require that insurance companies cover the procedure. Several states, including Arkansas, Hawaii, Maryland, Massachusetts, and

Texas, have already introduced such legislation. However, one must question whether this is the best approach because legislation will not necessarily promote accountability; it merely mandates funding.

We believe that accountability and legislation should go hand in hand; neither approach would be entirely successful alone. But it will not be easy to accomplish these changes. Convincing insurance companies that it is in their own best interests to fund accredited IVF programs will be a long, slow process. On the other hand, insurance companies that are forced to fund programs with widely varying results could be expected to support repeal of that mandate in the next legislative session. Therefore, the quickest and most effective way to make IVF affordable to the majority of the American public depends on dual accountability by the medical profession and insurance industry, legislative mandate, and consumer pressure.

Accreditation of IVF Programs Would Benefit Infertile Couples and the Medical Profession

Central to the entire issue of inequitable insurance reimbursement policies for IVF and related advanced reproductive technologies is the concept of accountability—by the medical profession in regard to reported success rates and by the insurance industry with respect to funding procedures performed by IVF and related programs that meet "acceptable standards."

We believe that such accountability can be achieved through the establishment of an independent accrediting body. Such an accrediting body might seek participation, advice, and financial assistance from industries that market fertility-related medications, diagnostics, and equipment; the insurance industry; IVF and related programs; infertility-oriented consumer groups; and perhaps even from various levels of government. This body might work closely with the American Fertility Society, SART, and the American College of Obstetricians and Gynecologists, all of which have already addressed the issue of operational standards as they should pertain to IVF and related technologies.

Although "acceptable standards of outcome" are difficult to quantify, the IVF success rates published in the journal *Fertility and Sterility* in 1988 by the Medical Research Institute (MRI) and SART provide at least a starting point. The MRI/SART report, which presents the experience of 41 IVF programs registered by SART in 1986, suggests a 17 percent nationwide average clinical pregnancy rate per embryo transfer in 1986. This extrapolates to a clinical pregnancy rate per egg retrieval of about 15 percent (based on the approximately 15 percent failure rate to reach embryo transfer because fertilization did not occur or no eggs were retrieved).

When one considers that approximately one-third of IVF pregnancies are likely to be lost along the way because of miscarriage, ectopic pregnancy, or perinatal death, this figure translates to about a 10 percent birthrate per egg retrieval performed by the forty-one programs cited. Accordingly, a clinical pregnancy rate per egg retrieval of 15 percent and an actual birthrate per egg retrieval of 10 percent might be considered "acceptable standards" for measuring success with IVF.

While the clinical pregnancy rate per egg retrieval is an indicator of an IVF program's proficiency, it is the birthrate per egg retrieval statistic that is most meaningful to consumers because it best predicts the outcome they might realistically expect (the actual "baby take-home rate" per egg recovery).

Under the system we propose, IVF programs might submit themselves to an ongoing process of peer review. Participating programs would register each prospective patient with the accrediting body prior to initiation of treatment; a patient code number could ensure confidentiality, and registration of the patient with the society would guarantee proper data interpretation.

Programs that initially submit themselves for accreditation would have 12 months to demonstrate they are indeed able to meet "acceptable standards." (Data from previous years would not be considered.) Programs wishing to apply for accreditation after the first year could submit to a similar prospective evaluation or might alternatively elect to undergo a detailed retrospective audit according to the standards set forth by the accrediting body's peer review committee. Instead of eliminating marginal IVF programs, which might occur as a result of government-mandated regulation, such an accrediting body would set an example and even help struggling programs upgrade their standards and performance in the area of high-tech infertility treatments.

Each accredited program would undergo an annual peer review to become reaccredited. This would provide an ongoing assurance of proficiency to the consumer and to the referring doctor and would also give each program important information regarding its own performance.

The attainment of accreditation by a particular program might prompt insurance companies to reimburse for IVF and related procedures performed in that setting. It is anticipated that participation in such an accrediting process would snowball as IVF programs become convinced accreditation would be in their own best interest for the sake of insurance reimbursement and to offset mandatory regulation by federal or state governments.

In our opinion, the current IVF registry sponsored by the SART represents an admirable but yet relatively inadequate effort to achieve quality assurance and set standards for IVF and related programs in this country. The lack of a peer review system for reported results perpetuates questions about the credibility of the data submitted and does nothing to dispel suspicion by both the medical profession and infertile couples regarding reported success rates. Moreover, the IVF registry does not provide either the consumer or the referring physician access to information regarding the location of successful IVF programs.

We envision that an accrediting body such as that just described, by promoting open accountability and full disclosure to patients by IVF programs in the hope of promoting rational expectations, will eliminate the aura of skepticism that currently threatens the existence and growth of this valuable infertility technology.

IVF Consumers Have an *Obligation* to Get Involved

Ultimately, consumers determine the quality of anything they get in life. They may have to band together to make their voices heard against the forces of the marketplace, but they can bring about change. Now is the time to be outspoken; if consumers do not participate in the campaign to put the IVF house in order, they have only themselves to blame if progress comes slowly. One of the most promising lobbying avenues would be to join one of the infertility support groups, both to become more informed and to speak with a larger voice before the medical profession, legislative groups, and the insurance industry.

It is time for consumers to marshal their buying power to demand that these "big A's" in the field of high-tech infertility management are met:

1. Accreditation of IVF programs on a voluntary basis;

2. Accountability by the medical profession with regard to providing validated statistics or a track record, and instilling rational expectations in infertile couples who seek their advice;

3. Availability and access to the consumer of state-of-the-art standards of care.

Some Orwellian Implications of Fertility Technology

What would George Orwell have said about new fertility technologies such as *cryopreserving* (freezing and storing in liquid nitrogen) eggs, sperm, and embryos for future use?

Cryopreservation as an Option: Frozen versus Fresh Semen

It has long been feasible to preserve semen by freezing. Only a few years ago, when a young male university student desired to raise some pocket money, he would produce a semen specimen and sell it to a physician who had a patient requiring artificial insemination by donor (AID). The physician would ask the student a few questions regarding his general health, the possibility of recent exposure to venereal diseases, and as to the likelihood of his carrying hereditary traits that might jeopardize any offspring. The student might then be examined, would undergo a few basic blood tests, and a simple semen analysis; and a few physical characteristics such as height, complexion, and eye and hair color would be documented.

But the use of fresh semen is no longer an acceptable option. Sperm banks still obtain semen specimens from students as well as other donors, but now they compile far more extensive background material on the donor, including a test for recent exposure to AIDS and to ensure that the man is not a carrier of the hepatitis-B virus. A masturbation specimen of semen is then frozen and stored for up to six months, at which time the AIDS antibody blood test is repeated. Only if the second test is negative can the sperm bank then safely release the specimen for use. The reason for this delay is that it can take several months for an individual infected with the AIDS virus to develop detectable amounts of antibodies in the blood.

The use of frozen semen impacts fertility treatment in several ways. First, freezing and transporting semen over long distances in liquid nitrogen canisters is far more costly than using a fresh specimen from a student. Secondly, although each specimen contains millions of sperm, a significant number die or lose their vitality and motility during the freezing and thawing process. However, even if half of the sperm in a semen specimen fail to survive cryopreservation, pregnancy can still occur because fertilization of an egg requires only one healthy sperm out of the millions contained within a specimen.

The pregnancy rate does, however, appear to be significantly lower with thawed semen than when a fresh specimen is used for artificial insemination. Yet in spite of these downsides, it is not only prudent but indeed highly advisable to avoid the use of fresh semen for artificial insemination and to deal directly with sperm cryopreservation banks that strictly observe the necessary typing and screening processes as well as the proper waiting period before issuing donor semen.

Because it is no longer feasible from a medico-legal, moral, and ethical point of view to safely use fresh donor semen, frozen semen is today the only option for all forms of donor insemination, regardless of whether intravaginal or intrauterine insemination, IVF, or GIFT is to be performed. A rare exception to this rule might be justified when a woman is insistent upon selecting her own donor. In such cases, both the patient and the donor should be fully informed of all the potential risks involved when fresh semen is used. The donor should undergo routine testing and evaluation, including tests for AIDS and hepatitis B; thereupon, the legal agreements necessary to protect all parties from frivolous litigation should be consummated before donor insemination is performed.

Embryo Freezing

Dramatic advances in the technology of embryo freezing and storing of human embryos for future use have exciting implications for IVF. In the past, most IVF laboratories performed embryo freezing (cryopreservation) only in selected cases where it was deemed that too many embryos had resulted from the IVF process than could safely be transferred to the woman's uterus. These leftover embryos, having undergone several stages of cleavage, were frozen once the embryo contained four to six blastomeres (reproductive cells). If the woman failed to conceive during the IVF cycle of treatment, or if she conceived and subsequently desired to attempt another conception, the embryos would be thawed at a selected time of a subsequent menstrual cycle, usually four or five days after the presumed time of ovulation, and would be transferred to the woman's uterus. This approach resulted in less than a 5 percent birth rate per embryo transfer.

Because each blastomere in the early embryo is potentially able to grow into a baby, it was previously considered advisable to allow the embryo to divide several times before freezing and banking it. It was believed that this approach would compensate for the high reproductive cell attrition rate that occurs during the freezing and thawing process. (As explained in Chapter 2, once the embryo has divided beyond the thirty-cell blastomere stage, approximately five to six days after fertilization, the reproductive cells lose their individual totipotentiality and begin to differentiate into specific organs and tissues for the developing baby).

Recent evidence strongly suggests that there may be significant advantages to freezing zygotes (the fertilized eggs that have not yet undergone cleavage) or embryos that are at the earliest possible stage of cleavage. These embryos would then be thawed at the appropriate time, cultured in order to ascertain their potential for subsequent cleavage, and would then be transferred to the woman's uterus about forty to fifty hours after ovulation (at a much earlier stage in the menstrual cycle than had previously been the case).

The downside of freezing zygotes or embryos consisting of two blastomeres is that 30 to 50 percent of all cryopreserved reproductive cells, whether blastomeres or zygotes, may be destroyed during the freezing process. Accordingly, the chances are potentially greater that single-celled zygotes or two-celled embryos would be totally destroyed by freezing than would be the case when embryos that have reached a more advanced stage of cleavage are frozen. The process of embryo freezing requires the use of cryoprotectants which protect reproductive cells from destruction during the freezing process. Glycerol and dimethylsulfoxide (DMSO) are two cryoprotectants that were commonly used in the past. Recent evidence strongly

suggests that use of propanediol as a cryoprotectant significantly reduces the reproductive cell attrition rate associated
with embryo freezing and may thereby significantly improve
the chances of zygotes or early embryos surviving the cryopreservation process.

These new advances in embryo freezing research offer great
hope for the future. Successful pregnancy rates of between 15
and 25 percent are now being reported following the transfer
of one or two thawed embryos into a woman's uterus, thereby
potentially providing the infertile couple with several oppor-
tunities to conceive, following the single performance of an
egg retrieval procedure.

The time may well arrive when a woman, well stimulated with
fertility agents so as to achieve the development of the maximum number of healthy follicles would undergo a single ultrasound-directed egg retrieval procedure under local or light
general anesthesia and the eggs would be fertilized in vitro. A
few embryos might be transferred into the woman's uterus one
or two days later, while the remaining zygotes or early embryos would be frozen, banked, and subsequently thawed in
preparation for embryo transfer during one or more subsequent
menstrual cycles. Such a month-by-month phased approach
is now favored because it is widely believed that there may be
significant benefits in transferring human embryos into a woman's uterus during natural cycles where fertility agents are
not administered or during cycles where fertility agents are selectively administered but the egg retrieval procedure is not
performed.

We believe that cryopreservation technology will continue
to advance rapidly and that the discovery of improved cryoprotectants, coupled with the ability to determine with greater
precision the most ideal time for replacing thawed embryos
into a woman's uterus, will contribute significantly to the treatment of infertility in general and to success rates following IVF
in particular.

Egg Freezing

At the time this book was written, a number of successful births had resulted from the transfer into a woman's uterus of an embryo or embryos derived from the in vitro fertilization of a previously frozen and then thawed human egg. It is, however, technically far more difficult to cryopreserve human eggs than embryos or sperm, and egg freezing technology is still in its infancy. There is currently a far greater attrition rate during the freezing and thawing of human eggs than is the case for sperm or even for human embryos. This is particularly significant because a woman capable of producing only a limited number of eggs per cycle can ill afford to lose most of them during cryopreservation, while a vast number of sperm survive even though many others die during freezing. In addition, eggs are usually subjected to IVF during the same cycle of treatment in which they are retrieved, and it is unlikely that more than three or four eggs from any one couple would be left over and available for freezing after egg retrieval.

One of the reasons eggs are so much more sensitive to cryopreservation than are sperm is because of the strikingly different composition of the two gametes. Sperm are comprised primarily of a head and a tail, with the head containing all nuclear (genetic) material. The egg, although vastly smaller, has a structure not dissimilar to that of a chicken egg. As with the chicken egg, where the nuclear material is far smaller than the white, or ooplasm, the human egg is also almost all ooplasm. The ooplasm contains the tiny microorganelles that nourish the fertilized egg and probably even the sperm once it has penetrated the egg after fertilization.

Eggs are particularly sensitive to cryopreservation because freezing and thawing can produce two effects:

1. The fluid contained within the microorganelles in the ooplasm might expand during freezing, rupturing the microorganelles' membrane walls and thereby disrupting the metabolic processes within the egg. In

contrast, the nuclear material that largely comprises most of each sperm appears to be relatively resistant to such damage.

2. The spindles from which chromosomes hang and that are indispensable to the exchange of genetic material during fertilization can be damaged when eggs are frozen and thawed. Spindle breakage could therefore potentially lead to an abnormal arrangement of chromosomes following fertilization.

However, nature is wisely selective. If an egg is defective, it almost certainly will not fertilize. If an embryo is defective, in the vast majority of cases it will not implant into the wall of the uterus and the woman will likely never know that she was pregnant in the first place. If the *conceptus* is damaged following implantation prior to the sixth to eighth week of pregnancy, the pregnancy will almost invariably abort. However, if an older conceptus or fetus is damaged, it becomes more likely that a birth defect might result. So, nature makes a gallant attempt to maintain the integrity of the species by preferring that defective gametes are incapable of fertilization, that defective embryos do not implant, and that imperfect conceptuses miscarry in the early stages of pregnancy.

Accordingly, an egg with defective ooplasm is highly unlikely to cause a problem, but the fact that spindle breakages have been observed following the thawing and fertilization of eggs has created some ambivalence on the part of many IVF specialists to apply this technology in humans.

Frozen Eggs versus Frozen Embryos

The present survival rate for embryos following thawing, based solely upon the observation that more than half of their cells appear to have weathered cryopreservation, is slightly greater than 50 percent. In contrast, the chances are now between 10 and 15 percent that an egg will survive the freezing process, with evidence of survival as demonstrated by subsequent apparently healthy cleavage. The recent introduction of newer methods promises to push this percentage up considerably in the foreseeable future. Although such numbers would seem to favor embryo freezing, we are convinced that egg freezing, thawing, and subsequent fertilization and embryo transfer will eventually prove to be far preferable to the use of embryos and will likely become standard practice in the IVF setting.

There are several advantages to cryopreserving eggs rather than embryos. First, an egg is a known quantity; it is likely to be healthy if it fertilizes and undergoes subsequent division or cleavage following thawing. On the other hand, because the embryo is often transferred to the uterus immediately after thawing without undergoing further cleavage, one does not usually have the opportunity to observe whether it is indeed healthy at the time of embryo transfer. Because the embryo is further along the chain of evolution than an egg, the potential that an embryo damaged through freezing and thawing would produce an abnormal offspring is greater than that which could be anticipated from an embryo derived from a previously thawed egg.

Second, egg freezing avoids the moral-ethical dilemma as to whether life in its earliest form is being manipulated. Eggs, like sperm, are considered to be cells that do not have life potential on their own. On the other hand, many people believe that an embryo represents the earliest form of life and that the high attrition rate of frozen-thawed embryos represents a form of abortion. However, the same argument cannot be applied to the freezing and thawing of eggs. If one were to argue that it is unethical to freeze an egg because its chance of survival and subsequent fertilization is questionable, then it should likewise be unethical to freeze semen because many of the sperm also die during cryopreservation. In this context it might also be argued that the normal practice of vaginal intercourse is wasteful because only one or two, and rarely three or four sperm might be capable of fertilizing eggs and producing offspring, and the remaining sperm would die. Thus, most people who have a religious or moral aversion to embryo freezing would be unlikely to have the same objection to the freezing of eggs.

Third, eggs are easier to obtain than embryos. A potential source of eggs could theoretically be women undergoing certain kinds of abdominal surgery. Such women could first be stimulated with fertility drugs, and their eggs could be retrieved at the same time that an unrelated form of surgery is being performed. The donor could then be reimbursed for donating her eggs to an egg bank or an awaiting recipient, and the payment received could help offset the cost of her surgery. Candidates might include women who undergo laparoscopy to have their fallopian tubes surgically occluded for the purpose of sterilization, women having hysterectomies for benign pelvic disease, or those undergoing diagnostic laparoscopies or diagnostic ultrasound examinations.

In addition, when more eggs are retrieved from a woman undergoing egg retrieval from IVF than the number necessary to optimize the likelihood that four to six embryos will be fertilized in the laboratory, the woman might choose to donate or sell these excess eggs to an egg bank or to other infertile women. We reject the sexist argument that it is immoral for women to sell their eggs while it is acceptable for men to sell their sperm.

Fourth, excess frozen eggs could be used to diagnose male fertility where the cause could not be otherwise diagnosed. It is possible to render such eggs unfertilizable by bisecting them or by aspirating their contents prior to performance of the male fertility test (see Chapter 8). By observing sperm interaction with bisected or aspirated eggs, laboratory personnel could determine whether the sperm are capable of attaching to or penetrating the surface of human eggs and, thus, whether the acrosome reaction (see Chapter 2) can take place.

In our opinion, the popularity of embryo freezing is ultimately likely to be upstaged by egg freezing. However, embryo freezing will always have a place in the IVF setting because it is likely, when large numbers of eggs are fertilized in the laboratory, that the couple will be left with more embryos than they or the IVF team would be willing to transfer into the woman's uterus. These excess embryos would either have to be allowed to die spontaneously or be frozen, stored, and kept available for a subsequent chance at conceiving should the initial IVF cycle be unsuccessful. However, we believe that with few exceptions egg cryopreservation will almost invariably be the better option in the future. As the technology continues to develop and be refined, egg cryopreservation should provide a variety of benefits to infertile couples.

Should New Fertility Technology Be Regulated?

What are some of the potential uses and abuses of new fertility technology? This new technology raises a host of moral and ethical issues that have yet to be resolved, and probably never will be answered to everyone's satisfaction. For example, animal studies have shown that it is possible to create new species through IVF by allowing fertilization to occur between gametes of different species. Fortunately, such new species are unlikely to have the potential to reproduce.

One or more blastomeres could also theoretically be injected into a zona whose contents had previously been removed, and the artificially produced embryo could then be transferred into a woman's uterus. It is even theoretically possible that human embryos could be nurtured in the uterus of another species.

Where does it end? To what extent should technology be allowed to alter the normal course of nature? It is now possible, by administering the proper hormones, to stimulate a woman who has a uterus but no ovaries, or a woman who may even be postmenopausal, to prepare her endometrium to receive an embryo. She could then carry to term and give birth to a child who began life as an embryo provided by two donors or a donor egg that had been fertilized by her partner. How late in a woman's life is she entitled to have a child? Should a woman of 50 or 60 who wants to have a baby be stimulated in this manner? We believe this procedure should be done with caution because of the ethical dilemmas it presents.

The following three examples were offered by the laboratory director of a major IVF program to illustrate the kinds of questions that he encounters.

A 28-year-old female medical student requested:

> Is it possible for you to freeze two or three stimulated cycles of my eggs now? I'll be over 35 by the time I get out of medical school, and I'd like to begin my family about age 40— but with age-28 eggs.

When a graduate student received widespread publicity after the birth of identical twin calves from a cow embryo he had split, a couple asked the laboratory director:

> Would you please split one of our embryos so we can have identical twins?

And a terminally ill man asked:

> My wife has agreed to bear me a large family after I'm gone. Would you freeze several samples of my sperm and artificially inseminate her over the years so she could have my family?

The director refused the requests, but he fully expects to be confronted with many more such requests in the future. Although addressing these dilemmas is not within the scope of this book, the examples mentioned in this chapter illustrate but a few of the moral and ethical dilemmas that arise with IVF and related technologies.

What about the positive side of this new technology? We are now capable of drilling a hole in the zona pellucida or of inducing enzyme digestion of a small area of the zona so as to create a minute window through which a single sperm might pass or be injected. This form of *gamete micromanipulation* offers great promise for the treatment of infertility due to severe sperm dysfunction. But many justifiable questions arise, for example: Should blastomeres that carry inherited diseases such as hemophilia or diabetes be combined with blastomeres that do not carry those traits to enable the embryo to select against such diseases? Should embryonic or fetal cells be injected into other embryos or fetuses to reverse the enzyme reactions that may be responsible for certain birth defects? Ultimately, society itself must determine whether technology should be allowed to run rampant or should be controlled. We recognize the widespread concern of the medical community that regulation of one aspect of medicine may lead to creeping regulation of the entire profession. Nevertheless, we believe it would be socially responsible to adopt, at the national level, directives or requirements that would control this developing technology for the public good.

The social responsibility that confronts practitioners of IVF and related technologies was underscored by Dr. Gary Hodgen, at an IVF conference in Reno:

> How can we in the area of in vitro fertilization do anything other than search and struggle together to find what this moral and ethical obligation is, define it, and attempt to refine it as we move forward with research results, technology, and new capabilities to help infertile couples?
>
> There is little difference of opinion in this pluralistic society about the needs of people to have well children. The issue that's at risk is how we get there—implementation of research and clinical care.

The time has come to move from recommendations and guidelines, inconsistently applied, to strong directives that can be enforced. Loosely stated guidelines do not provide enough guidance and leave the field wide open to abuse (all too often guidelines have been adopted because decision-makers are afraid to say "This is what you *will do*" and thus settle for "This is what we recommend you might do *if you want to*").

Decisions about the future directions of fertility technology cannot be left to one interest group. In our pluralistic society varying viewpoints and backgrounds must be represented in order to make the consensus process work: consumers, physicians and other practitioners of IVF, the clergy, fertility support groups, lawyers, insurance carriers, ethical specialists, the media, and legislators must all work together to bring about the national adoption of comprehensive, enforceable directives to guide the implementation of research and clinical care in the field of fertility.

Where Will IVF Be Performed in the Future?

After the initial shakeout period, the United States may have fewer IVF programs, but programs that are validated by peer review and offer a uniformly reliable success rate. Just because there are fewer programs, however, does not mean that access to IVF will be more difficult than it is now for consumers who do not live in metropolitan areas. On the contrary, mobile units may bring IVF and related procedures to the couple's own area, where they are familiar with the doctor and feel most comfortable.

For example, instead of twenty-five small programs in one geographical area, all of which have relatively high costs because they cannot benefit from economies of scale, consolidation and regionalization might provide better service to the entire area. One large, well-equipped center could serve outlying communities as well as the metropolitan area, reducing overhead costs while maintaining an optimal level of technology and research.

With support from such a regional center, IVF could eventually become a doctor's-office procedure. A medical team in the regional center could guarantee 24-hour consultation backup to rural doctors in regard to patient screening, stimulation procedures, embryo-transfer protocols, and other aspects of IVF. In addition, a central IVF laboratory could serve physicians within a large catchment territory.

Traveling physician's assistants or technologists trained in the specific nuances and intricacies of IVF could work with rural physicians in their own offices or local hospitals. The team might travel in a recreational vehicle converted into an IVF laboratory, on a schedule timed to coincide with egg retrievals that will be performed by local physicians. An IVF-trained technologist could even scrub in and assist during egg retrieval when the physician is not familiar with the actual procedure of sucking eggs out of the follicles.

Fertilization might take place in the mobile unit; or the mobile unit could transport the eggs to the regional center for fertilization and bring the embryos back for transfer. Carrying this idea even further, the same mobile unit might even be adapted for embryo transfer. Once successful IVF procedures can be replicated throughout the United States, mobile IVF may become the wave of the future.

Conclusion

- For the thousands of couples whose lives have been enriched by the gift of life through IVF and other assisted reproductive technologies;

- For the many more infertile couples who have little hope of conceiving without the assistance of these procedures;

- And mindful of the sacred doctrine that binds the medical profession to alleviate human suffering wherever possible;

We challenge the medical/scientific communities and consumers alike to strive together to expand the technology, improve the quality, and promote the affordability and accessibility of IVF and related technologies.

Glossary

Italicized terms are defined elsewhere in this glossary.

Acrosome: The protective structure around the head of the *sperm*. The acrosome contains enzymes that enable the sperm to penetrate the *egg*.

Acrosome reaction: The second stage of *capacitation,* when a *sperm* fuses with the *zona pellucida.*

Adrenal glands: Small structures located at the top of each kidney that produce a number of hormones indispensable to proper growth, development, and a wide variety of physiologic functions.

AID: See *artificial insemination by donor.*

AIDS: A sexually transmitted disease believed to be caused by one or a variety of viruses that are harbored in the *nuclei* of cells and attack the immune system. Infected individuals become highly susceptible to opportunistic infections; AIDS may ultimately lead to death.

American Fertility Society: A professional society whose membership comprises physicians, laboratory personnel, psychologists, nurses, and other paramedical personnel interested in infertility.

Antibodies to sperm: Substances in the man's or woman's blood and in reproductive secretions that reduce fertility by causing *sperm* to stick together, coating their surface, or killing them.

Anus: Excretory opening of the intestinal tract.

Artificial insemination by donor (AID): The most common form of *insemination* into the *vagina;* AID involves the use of donor *semen* or *sperm* in cases where the woman's partner is infertile or the woman chooses to conceive without the participation of a chosen partner.

Augmented laparoscopy: A procedure in which eggs are retrieved from the woman's *ovaries* while a *diagnostic laparoscopy* is being performed to evaluate the integrity of her pelvic organs. These eggs are subsequently fertilized *in vitro,* and the *embryos* are transferred into the woman's *uterus* two or three days later. This procedure affords a woman undergoing routine diagnostic laparoscopy a chance to determine the cause of her *infertility* and an opportunity to conceive by *IVF* at the same time.

Basal body temperature (BBT) chart: A daily body temperature chart that provides a rough idea when *ovulation* occurred. This is possible because body temperature rises when the *corpus luteum* produces *progesterone* (after ovulation) and drops at or just before the beginning of *menstruation,* when estrogen and progesterone levels fall (see also *biphasic pattern of temperature on BBT chart*).

BBT chart: See *basal body temperature chart.*

Billings Method of contraception: A method of predicting *ovulation* where the woman examines the quality and quantity of her own *cervical mucus* secretions; this method can be used to help the woman determine her most fertile period for the purpose of conceiving or for contraception.

Biphasic pattern of temperature on BBT chart: Charting pattern that occurs because the woman's temperature during the first phase of her *menstrual cycle* is likely to be ½° to 1° lower than during the second half, when the *progesterone* produced by the *corpus luteum* raises her temperature slightly (see also *basal body temperature chart*).

Bladder: The anatomical reservoir that receives urine produced by the kidneys.

Blastocyst: The stage at which a cavity develops within the young *embryo*.

Blastomere: Cell within the developing *embryo*. Each blastomere is capable of developing into an identical embryo until the embryo reaches about the thirty-cell stage, after which time the cells begin to differentiate into specific tissues.

Blood-hormone test—LH: When this test is performed several times daily around the presumed time of *ovulation*, the detection of a rapidly rising blood *LH* concentration can accurately determine the time of probable ovulation. This test, which requires blood to be drawn several times and is therefore painful, time-consuming, and expensive, has been virtually supplanted by serial urine LH testing (see also *urine ovulation test*).

Blood-hormone test—progesterone: Measuring the concentration of *progesterone* in the woman's blood during the second half of the *menstrual cycle* prior to anticipated *menstruation* indicates whether or not she is likely to have ovulated because progesterone is usually only produced by the *corpus luteum,* which develops after *ovulation*.

Capacitation: The process by which sperm are prepared for *fertilization* as they pass through the woman's reproductive tract (*in vivo* capacitation); sperm may also be capacitated in the laboratory (*in vitro* capacitation).

Cervical canal: The connection between the outer cervical opening and the uterine cavity.

Cervical mucus: Mucus produced by glands in the *cervical canal;* this mucus plays an important role in initiating the *capacitation* of *sperm*.

Cervical mucus insufficiency: A condition where the ability of the *cervical mucus* to initiate the *capacitation* process is compromised through a deficiency in the amount of mucus produced, an abnormality in the physical-chemical components of the mucus, the presence of infection, an abnormal hormonal environment, or the secretion of *antibodies to sperm* in the mucus. Cervical mucus insufficiency is responsible for about 10 percent of all cases of *infertility*.

Cervix: Lowermost part of the *uterus,* which protrudes like a bottleneck into the upper *vagina;* the cervix opens into the uterus through the narrow *cervical canal.*

Chemical pregnancy: Biochemical evidence of a possible developing pregnancy based on a positive blood or urine pregnancy test; at this point, pregnancy is presumptive until confirmed by *ultrasound* (see also *clinical pregnancy*).

Chlamydia: Bacteria that are responsible for a sexually transmitted infection that may damage the *fallopian tubes* and/or the male reproductive ducts, thereby causing *infertility*.

Chromosomes: Structures in the *nuclei* of cells, such as the *egg* and *sperm,* on which the hereditary or genetic material is arrayed.

Cleavage: The process of cell division.

Climacteric: The hormonal change that precedes the *menopause* by a number of years and is associated with a progressive loss of fertility, an increased incidence of abnormal or absent *ovulation,* hot flashes, irregular *menstruation,* and mood changes. The climacteric usually represents an important stage of emotional reevaluation in a woman's life.

Clinical pregnancy: A pregnancy that has been confirmed by ultrasonic examination or through pathologic examination of a surgical specimen obtained either from a *miscarriage* or from an *ectopic pregnancy.* A clinical pregnancy should be distinguished from a *chemical pregnancy,* which through a positive blood pregnancy test merely suggests the possibility that a pregnancy has occurred.

Clitoris: The small structure at the junction of the *labia minora* in front of the *vulva.* The clitoris, which is analogous to the *penis* in the male, undergoes erection during erotic stimulation and plays an important role in orgasm.

Clomiphene citrate: A synthetic *hormone* that is used alone or in combination with other fertility drugs to induce the *ovulation* of more than one *egg.*

COH: See *controlled ovarian hyperstimulation.*

Conception: Creation of a *zygote* by the *fertilization* of an *egg* by a *sperm.*

Conceptus: A term used to describe the developing implanted *embryo* and/or early *fetus.*

Controlled ovarian hyperstimulation (COH): In response to the administration of *fertility drugs,* the maturation of several *follicles* simultaneously, which results in the production of an exaggerated hormonal response.

Corona radiata: See *cumulus mass.*

Corpus luteum: A term for a follicle after an egg has been extruded. After *ovulation,* the follicle collapses, turns yellow, and is transformed biochemically and hormonally. The corpus luteum produces *progesterone* and *estrogen* and has a lifespan of about 10 to 14 days, after which it dies unless a pregnancy occurs. If the woman becomes pregnant the lifespan of the corpus luteum is prolonged for many weeks. A synonym for the corpus luteum is the *"yellow body."*

Cul-de-sac: Area of the woman's abdominal cavity behind the lower part of the *uterus.*

Cumulus mass: The group of cells resembling a sunburst that surround the *zona pellucida* of the human *egg;* also called the *corona radiata.*

Cryopreservation: The process of freezing in liquid nitrogen and storing *eggs, sperm,* and *embryos* for future use.

de Miranda Institute: A consumer protection agency for infertile couples, located in Bedford, Texas.

DES (diethylstilbestrol): A drug previously taken by women during pregnancy that may cause *infertility* and/or pathologic conditions in the reproductive tracts of both male and female offspring.

Diagnostic IVF: See *augmented laparoscopy.*

E$_2$: See *estradiol.*

Ectopic pregnancy: A pregnancy that occurs when the *embryo* attempts to implant in a location other than the *uterus;* the most common site for such implantation is the *fallopian tube* (in which case the term ectopic pregnancy is used synonymously with *tubal pregnancy*). If undetected, an ectopic pregnancy may rupture and cause life-threatening internal bleeding; ectopic pregnancies almost always require surgical intervention.

Egg: The female *gamete,* which develops in the *ovary;* also known as an *ovum* or *oocyte.* An egg is the largest cell in the human body.

Egg retrieval: The retrieval of *eggs* from the ovarian *follicles* prior to *ovulation;* the eggs are sucked out of the follicles through a needle either during *laparoscopy* or under *ultrasound* guidance.

Ejaculation: The emission of *semen* through the *urethra* and *penis* that follows erotic stimulation and accompanies male orgasm.

Embryo: The term for a fertilized *egg* from the time of initial cell division through the first six to eight weeks of *gestation.* Thereafter, the embryo begins to differentiate and take on a human organic form; at this point it is traditionally referred to as a *fetus.*

Embryo adoption: This occurs when a woman receives into her *uterus* an *embryo* to which she has not contributed biologically; in many such cases neither the woman nor her partner will have contributed biologically to the embryo.

Embryo transfer: The process whereby *embryos* that have been grown *in vitro* are transferred into the *uterus.*

Endometrial biopsy: Surgical removal of a specimen of the *endometrium* commonly performed to enable microscopic examination of the effect of *estrogen* and *progesterone* on the endometrium. If this biopsy is performed by an expert, it is usually possible to pinpoint almost to the day when *ovulation* is likely to have occurred.

Endometriosis: A condition in which the *endometrium* grows outside the *uterus,* causing scarring, pain, and heavy bleeding, and often damaging the *fallopian tubes* and *ovaries* in the process. Endometriosis is a common organic cause of *infertility.*

Endometrium: The lining of the *uterus,* which grows during the *menstrual cycle* under the influence of *estrogen* and *progesterone.* The endometrium grows in anticipation of nurturing an implanting *em-*

bryo in the event of a *pregnancy;* it sloughs off in the form of *menstruation* if *implantation* does not occur.

Epididymis: Tubular reservoir that contains and transfers sperm to the *vas deferens* and subsequently through the *urethra* and *penis* at the time of ejaculation.

Estradiol (E$_2$): A female *hormone* produced by ovarian *follicles.* The concentration of *estrogen* in the woman's blood is often measured to determine the degree of her response to *controlled ovarian hyperstimulation* with *fertility drugs;* in general, the higher the estradiol response, the more *follicles* are likely to be developing and, accordingly, the more *eggs* are likely to be retrieved.

Estrogen: A primary female sex *hormone,* produced by the *ovaries, placenta,* and *adrenal glands.*

Exit interview: An interview prior to the couple's release from an *IVF* program after the performance of *embryo transfer, GIFT, artificial insemination,* or related procedures; an exit interview prepares the couple for their return home and provides valuable feedback to the program.

FSH: See *follicle-stimulating hormones.*

Fallopian tubes: Narrow 4-inch-long structures that lead from either side of the *uterus* to the *ovaries.*

Fertilization: The fusion of the *sperm* and *egg* to form a *zygote* (see also *zygote, conception*).

Fertility drugs: Natural or synthetic *hormones* that are administered to a woman in order to stimulate her *ovaries* to produce as many mature *eggs* as possible or to a man in an attempt to enhance *sperm* function.

Fetus: Once the *embryo* differentiates and begins to take on identifiable human-like organic form, it is termed a fetus; the fetal stage of development usually begins around the eighth week of pregnancy.

Fibroid tumor: A tumor in the *uterus,* which may prevent the *embryo* from properly *implanting* into the *endometrium* or might cause pain, bleeding, miscarriage, and symptomatic enlargement of the uterus.

Fibrous bands: Scar tissue that may distort the interior of the *uterus* and prevent the *embryo* from *implanting* properly.

Fimbriae: Finger-like protrusions from the ends of the *fallopian tubes* that retrieve the *egg* or eggs at the time of *ovulation*.

Follicles: Blister-like structures within the *ovary* that contain *eggs* and that produce female sex *hormones*.

Follicle-stimulating hormone (FSH): A *gonadotropin* that is released by the *pituitary gland* to stimulate the *ovaries* or *testicles*.

Follicular phase insufficiency or defect: An abnormal pattern of *estrogen* production during the first half of the *menstrual cycle*, which could result in *infertility* or recurrent *miscarriages* (should pregnancy occur).

Follicular phase of the menstrual cycle: See *proliferative phase of the menstrual cycle*.

Fornix (pl. fornices): Deep recesses in the upper *vagina* created by the protrusion of the *cervix* into the roof of the vagina.

FSH: *See follicle-stimulating hormone.*

Gamete: The female *egg* and the male *sperm*.

Gamete intrafallopian transfer (GIFT): A *therapeutic gamete-related technique* that involves the injection of one or more *eggs* mixed with *washed, capacitated,* and incubated *sperm* directly into the *fallopian tube(s)* in the hope that *fertilization* will occur *in vivo* and that a healthy pregnancy will follow.

Gamete micromanipulation: A special procedure performed on the gametes to promote in vitro fertilization in cases where there is severe sperm dysfunction.

Gastrulation: The stage of embryonic development when *blastomeres* are dedicated to the development of specific organs and structures.

Gestation: The period from *conception* to delivery.

GIFT: See *gamete intrafallopian transfer*.

GnRH: See *gonadotropin-releasing hormone*.

GnRH agonists: GnRH-like *hormones* that block the body's release of both *FSH* and *LH*. Through blocking LH production, GnRH agonists are capable of improving a woman's response to *fertility drugs* and may be used in combination with fertility drugs to promote an enhanced response in women who demonstrate resistance to *controlled ovarian hyperstimulation.*

Gonads: The *ovaries* and *testicles.*

Gonadotropin-releasing hormone (GnRH): A "messenger *hormone*" released by the *hypothalamus* to influence the production of *gonadotropins* by the *pituitary gland.*

Gonadotropins: The *gonad*-stimulating *hormones LH* and *FSH*, which are released by the *pituitary gland* to stimulate the *testicles* in the man and *ovaries* in the woman.

Gonococcus: A bacterium producing *gonorrhea*, a common venereal disease occurring in both men and women that may cause sterility.

Gonorrhea: A common venereal disease that may cause sterility in both men and women.

Growth medium: A physiological solution that promotes *cleavage* and development of the *embryo.*

hCG: See *human chorionic gonadotropin.*

Heparin: A drug that may be added to the solution used to flush *eggs* out of ovarian *follicles* during *egg retrieval;* its purpose is to prevent blood clotting within the fluid that harbors the egg.

hMG: See *human menopausal gonadotropin.*

Hormonal insufficiency: A condition resulting in *infertility* and/or *miscarriage;* in the *IVF* setting, hormonal insufficiency may be produced by an abnormal response to *fertility drugs* and may lead to the failure of an *embryo* to *implant* because the amount of *hormones* produced and the timing of their production and release were not perfectly synchronized.

Hormone (sex hormone): Chemicals produced by the *testicles, ovaries,* and *adrenal glands,* which play a major role in reproduction and sexual identity.

HSG: See *hysterosalpingogram.*

Hühner Test: See *postcoital test.*

Human chorionic gonadotropin (hCG): A *hormone*, produced by the implanting *embryo,* (and subsequently also by the *placenta*), whose presence in the woman's blood indicates a possible pregnancy; hCG may also be administered to women undergoing *stimulation* with *hMG* alone or in combination with other *fertility drugs* in order to trigger *ovulation*. Injections of hCG may also be administered to encourage the production of *progesterone* by the *corpus luteum* in the hope of promoting *implantation* following *embryo transfer* and thereby reducing the incidence of *spontaneous miscarriage* in a pregnancy resulting from *IVF*. The hormone hCG is derived from the urine of pregnant women.

Human menopausal gonadotropin (hMG): A natural *hormone* that is administered either alone or in combination with other *fertility drugs* to induce *ovulation* of more than one *egg*. The hormone hMG is derived from the urine of *menopausal* women.

Hypothalamus: A small area in the midportion of the brain that, together with the *pituitary gland,* regulates the formation and release of many *hormones* in the body, including *estrogen* and *progesterone* by the *ovaries* and *testosterone* by the *testes*.

Hysterosalpingogram (HSG): A procedure used to assess the interior of the *fallopian tubes* and *uterus;* it involves injecting a radioopaque dye into the uterus via the *vagina* and *cervix* and tracking the dye's pathway by a series of X-rays.

Hysteroscope: A lighted, telescope-like instrument that is passed through the *cervix* into the *uterus,* enabling the surgeon to examine the *cervical canal* and the inside of the uterus for defects or disease.

Hysteroscopy: Examination of the *cervical canal* and inside of the *uterus* for defects by means of the *hysteroscope*. Surgery designed to correct such defects can be performed through the hysteroscope during this procedure, thereby often making more *invasive* abdominal surgery unnecessary.

Implantation: The process that occurs when the *embryo* burrows into the *endometrium* and eventually connects to the mother's circulatory system.

In vitro fertilization (IVF or IVF/ET): Literally "*fertilization* in glass," IVF comprises several basic steps: the woman is given *fertility drugs* that *stimulate* her *ovaries* to produce a number of mature *eggs;* at the proper time, the eggs are retrieved by suction through a needle that has been inserted into her ovaries; the eggs are fertilized in a glass petri dish, or in a test tube, in the laboratory with her partner's or donor *sperm;* and subsequently the *embryos* are transferred into the *uterus.*

In vivo fertilization: *Fertilization* inside the body.

Inclusive pregnancy rates: Pregnancy success reports that combine rates for both *clinical* and *chemical* pregnancies and do not distinguish between the two.

Infertility: The inability to *conceive* after one full year of normal, regular heterosexual intercourse without the use of contraception.

Insemination: In the laboratory, the addition of a drop or two of the medium containing *capacitated sperm* to a petri dish containing the *egg* in order to achieve *fertilization;* also refers to placement of sperm into the woman's reproductive tract.

Insemination medium: A liquid that bathes and nourishes the *eggs* and *embryos* in the petri dish just as the mother's body fluids sustains them in nature; it may contain blood obtained from the woman or from a donor, or fetal umbilical cord blood obtained from the obstetric ward of a local hospital.

Intrauterine insemination (IUI): The injection of *sperm* (rarely *semen*) into the *uterus* by means of a catheter directed through the *cervix;* enables sperm of poor quality to reach and fertilize the egg more easily or to bypass hostile *cervical mucus.*

Intravaginal insemination (IVI): The injection of *semen* (usually donor semen) into the *vagina* in direct proximity to the *cervix* in the hope that pregnancy will occur.

Invasive procedure: In the case of fertility-related treatments, a surgical procedure that requires that one or more incisions be made in the woman's abdomen.

Iso-hormones: Similarly structured components that have different levels of biological activity; the influence of iso-hormones may be responsible for the variations in potency among different batches of gonadotropins such as *hMG* and purified *FSH.*

IUI: See *intrauterine insemination.*

IVF or IVF/ET: See *in vitro fertilization.*

IVI: See *intravaginal insemination.*

Knee-chest position: Position the woman may be asked to assume during *embryo transfer* if the *uterus* is tipped forward so as to contribute to optimal placement of the *embryos.*

Labia majora: The hair-covered outer lips of the external portion of the female reproductive tract.

Labia minora: The small inner lips of the outer female reproductive tract, partially hidden by the *labia majora.*

Laparoscope: A long, thin telescope-like instrument containing a high-intensity light source and a system of lenses that enable the surgeon to examine the abdominal cavity and to perform other diagnostic or surgical procedures under direct vision without necessitating major surgery.

Laparoscopy: A surgical procedure using the *laparoscope.* Laparoscopy may be used for *egg retrieval,* diagnostic evaluation, reparative surgery, and various other fertility procedures; because of its dual abilities to enable the physician to assess tubal *patency* and visualize the abdominal cavity, laparoscopy has largely replaced the *hysterosalpingogram* as the most popular method of assessing the anatomical integrity of the reproductive tract (see also *augmented laparoscopy*).

LH: See *luteinizing hormone.*

Lithotomy: Position that a woman is asked to assume in order to undergo a gynecological examination or other procedures such as *embryo transfer,* vaginal *ultrasound* examinations, etc.

Luteal-phase insufficiency or defect: The inadequate production of *hormones* during the second phase of the *menstrual cycle,* which may result in *infertility* or *miscarriage.*

Luteal phase of the menstrual cycle: See *secretory phase of the menstrual cycle.*

Luteinizing hormone (LH): A *gonadotropin* released by the *pituitary gland* to stimulate the *ovaries* and *testicles.*

Male subfertility: Less than optimal *sperm* quality, including configuration, *motility,* and count (number produced in a *semen* specimen).

Meiosis: The process of reducing and dividing the chromosomes in both the *sperm* and *egg,* which occurs immediately prior to and during *fertilization.*

Menopause: The period of a woman's life that begins with the total cessation of *menstruation,* usually between the ages of 40 and 55.

Menstrual cycle: The time that elapses between *menstrual periods.* The average cycle is 28 days, with *ovulation* usually occurring at the midpoint (around the fourteenth day).

Menstrual periods: See *menstruation.*

Menstruation: The monthly flow of blood when pregnancy does not occur; the flow comprises about two-thirds of the *endometrium* and blood, often including the unfertilized *egg* or unimplanted *embryo.*

Microorganelles: Tiny intracellular factories that produce energy and perform metabolic functions in the *egg,* where the microorganelles are located largely in the *ooplasm.*

Mini-laparotomy: A surgical procedure in which a 1 to 1½ inch incision is made in the abdomen above the pubic bone; it is used by some to facilitate the performance of *GIFT.*

Miscarriage: Spontaneous expulsion of the products of *conception* from the *uterus* in the first half of pregnancy.

Mitosis: The identical replication of cells by *cleavage;* mitosis is the process responsible for the growth and development of all tissues.

Morula: An early phase during which the developing *embryo,* which contains a large number of *blastomeres,* resembles a mulberry.

Motility (sperm motility): The ability of *sperm* to move and progress forward through the reproductive tract and fertilize the *egg;* sperm motility can be assessed microscopically.

Multiple pregnancy: The presence of more than one *gestation* within the *woman's reproductive tract* at the same time.

Myceles: Microfibers within the *cervical mucus* that *sperm* must swim through to reach the *uterus;* the woman's hormonal environment determines whether the arrangement of the myceles will facilitate or inhibit passage of the sperm. Around the time of *ovulation* the myceles are arranged in a parallel fashion so that sperm can swim between them in order to reach the uterus; it is believed that *capacitation* is initiated during that process.

Nucleus: Structure in the cell that bears the *chromosomes*.

Oocyte: See *egg*.

Ooplasm: Nurturing material around the *nucleus* in the *egg* that contains *microorganelles* and nurtures the *zygote* and *embryo* after *fertilization*.

Operative laparoscope: A *laparoscope* that has been modified to allow passage of a double-bore needle or surgical instruments through a groove or sleeve adjacent to the instrument (see also *laparoscope*).

Ovaries: Two white, almond-like structures, the female counterpart of the *testicles,* that are attached to each side of the pelvis adjacent to the ends of the *fallopian tubes;* the ovaries both release *eggs* and discharge sex *hormones* into the bloodstream.

Ovulation: The process that occurs when an *ovary* releases one or more *eggs*.

Ovum: See *egg*.

Patency: Openness, freedom from blockage (particularly referring to the *fallopian tubes*).

PCT test: See *postcoital test*.

Peeling: Removal of the *corona radiata* from the *embryo* by flushing the embryo through a syringe or pipette, or by microdissection using fine instruments. An embryo usually must first be peeled before it is possible to determine whether *fertilization* and *cleavage* have occurred.

Penis: The male external sex organ.

Perineum: The outer portion of the fibro-muscular wall and skin that separate the anus and *rectum* from the *vagina* and *vulva*.

Peritoneal cavity: The abdominal cavity that contains pelvic organs, bowel, stomach, liver, kidneys, *adrenal glands,* spleen, etc., and is lined by a membrane called the peritoneum.

Perivitelline membrane: Membrane that separates the *ooplasm* and *nuclear* material from the *zona pellucida* in the human *egg.*

Phrenic nerve: Nerve that may be irritated by trapped gas or blood during *laparoscopy* or following internal bleeding, resulting in subsequent pain in the shoulder, arm, and neck.

Pituitary gland: A small, grape-like structure hanging from the base of the brain that, together with the *hypothalamus,* produces and regulates the release of many *hormones* in the body.

Placenta: The factory that nourishes the *fetus* throughout pregnancy and is connected to the baby's belly button via the umbilical cord.

Placentation: Formation and attachment of the *placenta* to the *uterine* wall.

Plasma membrane: Double-layered membrane that envelops the entire sperm.

Polycystic ovarian disease: Condition in which the *ovaries* develop multiple small cysts; it is often associated with abnormal or absent *ovulation* and, accordingly, with *infertility.*

Polyps (uterine): Outgrowths that protrude into the *uterus* and may cause pain and bleeding or prevent an *embryo* from *implanting.*

Polyspermia: The entry of more than one *sperm* into an *egg* during *fertilization;* this causes the *zygote* to die or the *embryo* to divide haphazardly and then die.

Postcoital (PCT) test: Assessment of the *cervical mucus* after intercourse to evaluate the quality of the mucus and mucus-*sperm* interaction; also known as the *Hühner Test.*

Pregnancy-specific glycoprotein (SP-1): A *hormone* that appears in the blood only a few days later than *hCG* during pregnancy. May be measured instead of hCG to diagnose pregnancy.

Progesterone: A primary female sex *hormone* produced by the *corpus luteum* that induces secretory changes in the glands of the *endometrium.* Progesterone may also be given by injection or in the form of vaginal suppositories to enhance *implantation* and reduce the risk of *miscarriage*.

Prolactin: A hormone produced by the brain that influences the activity of *FSH* on the *ovaries*.

Proliferative phase of the menstrual cycle: Usually the first half of the *menstrual cycle*, when the *endometrium* proliferates under the influence of *estrogen* and the *follicles* develop; also known as the *follicular phase*.

Prostaglandins: Natural *hormones* contained in a multitude of cells in the body as well as in the *seminal fluid*. The placement of *semen*, which contains seminal fluid with prostaglandins, directly in the *uterus* in quantities greater than 0.2 ml can cause life-threatening shock.

Prostate gland: Gland in the male reproductive tract that secretes a milky substance that nurtures and promotes survival of *sperm*.

Purified FSH: A *fertility hormone* that is derived by processing and purifying *hMG* to eliminate the *LH* component.

Quantitative Beta hCG blood pregnancy test: Test that detects and measures the amount of *hCG* (produced by an *implanting embryo*) in the woman's blood. Measured eight to ten days after *embryo transfer*, it can diagnose a possible pregnancy before the woman has missed a *menstrual period*.

Rectum: Lower portion of the large intestine that connects to the *anal* canal.

Resolve, Inc.: One of the largest and most reputable fertility support groups in the United States; its national office is in Arlington, Massachusetts.

Retrograde ejaculation: A condition, sometimes caused by removal of a diseased *prostate gland*, in which the man *ejaculates* backward into the bladder rather than outward through the *penis*. It may cause *infertility* but can be treated by *inseminating* the woman with *sperm* separated from urine the man would pass immediately following orgasm.

SP-1: See *pregnancy-specific glycoprotein*.

Salpingoscopy: A procedure involving the introduction of a thin fiber-optic instrument into the *fallopian tube* or tubes to promote visualization of the tubal lining. It is usually performed during *laparoscopy* but may also be performed through a *hysteroscope*. Salpingoscopy facilitates diagnosis, surgery, or the placement of *eggs, sperm,* and *embryos* in order to foster pregnancy.

Salpingostomy: An operation in which the end of one or both *fallopian tubes* is opened surgically. Because this procedure involves removing all or part of the *fimbrial* end of the fallopian tube, it produces a relatively poor pregnancy rate for the infertile couple.

Scrotum: Pouch in which the male's *testicles* are suspended outside the body.

Secretory phase of the menstrual cycle: The second half of the *menstrual cycle,* which begins after *ovulation* under the influence of *estrogen* and *progesterone* produced by the *corpus luteum*; the term *secretory* is derived from the secretion by the *endometrium* of a substance that will sustain an *embryo;* also known as the *luteal phase.*

Selective reduction of pregnancy: Prior to completion of the third month of pregnancy, reduction of the number of *fetuses* in a large *multiple pregnancy* by injecting a chemical substance under *ultrasound* guidance; the fetus or fetuses succumb almost immediately and are absorbed by the body. It may be considered a life-saving measure to the remaining fetuses in high multiple pregnancies such as quadruplets, quintuplets, or greater and may reduce the risk of high multiple pregnancies to the mother.

Semen: The combination of *sperm, seminal fluid,* and other male reproductive secretions.

Seminal fluid: Milky fluid produced by the *seminal vesicles* that is ejaculated during erotic experiences (see also *semen*).

Seminal vesicles: Glands in the male reproductive tract that secrete a milky substance that nurtures and promotes survival of *sperm.*

Sperm: The male *gamete;* spermatozoa.

Sperm antibody test: Test that determines whether either partner's blood or the woman's *cervical mucus* contains *antibodies* to sperm.

Sperm count: A basic fertility-assessment test of *sperm* function, primarily involving counting the number of sperm, assessing their *motility* and progression, and evaluating their overall structure and form.

Spontaneous menstrual abortion: An early *miscarriage* occurring at the time of *menstruation* without the woman's *menstrual period* being delayed.

Sterility: See *infertility*.

Stimulation: Induction of the development of a number of *follicles* in response to the administration of *fertility drugs* (see also *controlled ovarian hyperstimulation* and *superovulation*).

Superovulation: The *ovulation* of more than one *egg* induced through the administration of *fertility drugs* (see also *controlled ovarian hyperstimulation* and *stimulation*).

Surrogation: When an infertile woman uses someone else's *uterus* to carry a child to term for her. Surrogation can be divided into (1) cases in which the surrogate mother contributes biologically to the offspring by providing her own *eggs,* or (2) when the surrogate does not contribute biologically—and therefore must undergo *IVF*.

Syphilis: A life-endangering venereal disease that in its late stages attacks most systems in the body, including the cardiovascular and central nervous systems.

Testes: See *testicles*.

Testicles: The male counterparts of the female *ovaries;* located in the *scrotum*, the testicles produce *sperm* and male hormones such as *testosterone*.

Testosterone: The predominant male sex *hormone*, which influences the production and maturation of *sperm*.

Therapeutic gamete-related technologies: Procedures involving the use of *gametes* to enhance the chances of *conception* through subsequent *insemination,* or transfer of *eggs* and/or *sperm* into the woman's *uterus, fallopian tubes,* or *peritoneal cavity*.

TPI: See *transperitoneal insemination*.

Transabdominal egg retrieval: An *ultrasound*-guided *egg retrieval* procedure in which the needle is passed through the abdominal wall and a full *bladder* into the *ovarian follicles;* has largely been surpassed by *transvaginal egg retrieval.*

Transurethral egg retrieval: An *ultrasound*-guided *egg retrieval* procedure in which the needle is passed through the *urethra* and the *bladder* wall into the *ovaries;* has largely been surpassed by *transvaginal egg retrieval.*

Transvaginal egg retrieval: An *ultrasound*-guided *egg retrieval* procedure in which the needle is passed through the back or side of the woman's *vagina* into her *ovaries.*

Transperitoneal insemination (TPI): The injection of *washed sperm* through a syringe into the woman's pelvic cavity at the time of expected *ovulation* to promote *conception;* may be combined with *intrauterine insemination.*

Treatment cycle: The *menstrual cycle* during which a particular fertility treatment such as *IVF, IUI, AID, GIFT*, etc. was performed.

Tubal pregnancy: See *ectopic pregnancy.*

Ultrasound: A painless diagnostic procedure that transforms high-frequency sound waves as they travel through body tissue and fluid into images on a TV-like screen; it enables the physician to clearly identify structures within the body and to guide instruments during certain procedures. Ultrasound is also used to diagnose a *clinical pregnancy.*

Unexplained infertility: Infertility whose cause cannot be readily determined by conventional diagnostic procedures; this occurs in about 10 percent of all infertile couples.

Urethra: The canal-like structure through which urine passes from the *bladder* and *semen* passes during ejaculation.

Urine ovulation test: A simple test that can pinpoint the time of presumed *ovulation;* frequent charting of the test results detects the surge of *LH* that triggers *ovulation.*

Uterus: A muscular organ that enlarges during pregnancy from its normal pear-like size to accommodate a full-term pregnancy.

Vagina: The narrow passage that leads from the *vulva* to the *cervix.* The *vagina's* elastic tissue, muscle, and skin have enormous ability to stretch so as to accommodate the *penis* during the sex act and the passage of a baby during childbirth.

Varicocele: A collection of dilated veins around the *testicles* that hinders *sperm* function, possibly through increasing the temperature in the *scrotum*.

Vas deferens: Tube that connects the *epididymis* with the *urethra* in the male reproductive tract.

Vasectomy: Surgery to block the male's *sperm* ducts for the purpose of birth control.

Vestibule: The cleft between the *labia minora;* the entrance to the *vagina*.

Vulva: The external portion of the female reproductive tract.

Washing (sperm washing): The processing of a *semen* specimen in a centrifuge in order to separate the *sperm* from the *semen* specimen.

Yellow body: See *corpus luteum*.

ZIFT: See *zygote intrafallopian transfer*.

Zona-cumulus complex: The mass of cells (*zona pellucida* and *cumulus mass*) through which the *sperm* must pass to reach the *egg*.

Zona-free hamster-egg penetration test: A technique that helps determine whether *sperm* are likely to fertilize healthy *eggs*.

Zona pellucida: The shell-like covering of the human *egg*.

Zygote: The term for a fertilized *egg* until it begins to *cleave*, at which time it is known as an *embryo*.

Zygote intrafallopian transfer (ZIFT): The placement of one or more *zygotes* into the outer third of the *fallopian tube(s)* during *laparoscopy* or *mini-laparotomy* in the hope that the resulting *embryo(s)* will travel to the *uterus* and implant successfully.

INDEX

In vivo fertilization (*Cont.*):
IVI, 165, 174, 186, 209
and surrogation, 173–175, 216
transperitoneal, 163–164, 166,
167, 217
ZIFT, 172–173, 218
Iso-hormones, 72, 74, 209
IUDs, 120, 124
IUI (*see* Intrauterine
insemination)
IVF (in vitro fertilization), xi,
xii, xiii, 8, 21, 27, 34, 35, 37,
41–49, 119, 124, 159, 166,
170, 172, 173, 188
and abnormalities, 44
acceptance into a program,
54–55
accessibility, 177–184
accreditation, 180–184
and age, 132–133
alternatives to, 159–175
and antibodies, 43
(*See also* Antibodies to
sperm)
best candidates for, 46–49
and birth rates, 151–152
and capacitation, 21, 43
(*See also* Cervix)
chances of success, 131–133,
139
and cervix, 43
consumers and standards,
176–184
costs, xviii–xix, 45, 54–55, 81,
125–126, 129, 135–143, 145,
163, 168, 176, 178–181
counseling on, 153
couples and programs,
distribution, 179–180
and cryopreservation, 185–193
diagnostic capability,
applications, 44–45, 88, 93,
94, 111, 122–123, 168, 171
distorted ideas about, xvi–xvii
egg retrieval (*see* Egg retrieval)
and embryo survival, 41, 100
embryo transfer (*see* Embryo
transfer)

IVF (in vitro fertilization) (*Cont.*):
emotional costs, 135–139, 140,
143, 145, 153
ethical objections, 62, 145,
175, 191–192, 193–196
and expectations, reasonable,
130–145
and fallopian tubes, 42, 44, 45
(*See also* Laparoscopy)
and female babies, 44
and fertility drugs (*see* Fertility
drugs)
and fertility tests, 111–120
and financial commitment,
140–143, 145
future programs, prospects,
196–197
and GIFT, 171–172
history and success, xv,
xvi–xvii
induction of ovulation, 55,
64–80, 132
information, obtaining, 154–158
insurance coverage, xii–xiii,
xviii–xix, 81, 88, 89, 125,
126, 140, 142–143, 163,
176, 179, 180–181, 183
IUI, 163
laboratory's role in, 90–95,
162
and meiosis and mitosis
problems, 34
men, evaluation of, 112–114
and menopause, proximity to,
46
and menstrual cycle (*see*
Menstrual cycle)
mobile units, 197
moral objections, 62, 145, 175,
191–192, 193–196
motivation to, 133–135
and multiple pregnancies, 42,
59, 97, 144
(*See also* Multiple
pregnancy)
and new species, 193
number of attempts, optimal,
143–144